·ICARUS·

The Boat that Flies

James Grogono

·ICARUS·

The Boat that Flies

ADLARD COLES LIMITED
8 Grafton Street, London W1

Adlard Coles Ltd
William Collins Sons & Co. Ltd
8 Grafton Street, London W1X 3LA

First published in Great Britain by
Adlard Coles Ltd 1987

Distributed in the United States of America
by Sheridan House, Inc.

British Library Cataloguing in Publication Data

Grogono, James
   Icarus: the boat that flies.
   1. Yacht racing   2. Hydrofoil boats
   I. Title
   797.1′4   GV826.5

ISBN 0-229-11803-8

Filmset in Great Britain by
BAS Printers Limited, Over Wallop, Hampshire

Printed and bound by
Butler and Tanner Ltd,
Frome, Somerset

To Catherine, Emma, Angus and Dorothy

Contents

Foreword

It is a platitude to say that one is honoured to introduce a book – any book. Of course it is.

Any book, indeed. But when the book is by a great sailor, a recognised expert and a long-time world speed record holder, then the honour becomes a pretty special one.

James Grog has been beating speed records year after year for the last fifteen years or so. He has notched up half a dozen ever-increasing records, as you will read.

He comes of a great sailing family – I've had trouble with them as long ago as the 1936 Olympics. I had lots of trouble with James himself in the Public Schools' team-racing in the '50s and '60s. Moreover he and I have also graced the same profession, though we made little contact there; he is a general surgeon, and I specialised in the opposite end.

His unchallengeable claim to fame is his imaginative development of hydrofoils, having first achieved mastery of dinghies, boards, monohulls, and the rest. He has not only made *Icarus* the quasi-permanent exemplar of the hydrofoil flier, but he has applied the hydrofoil to all sorts of other water-borne craft. He is in fact one of the great nautical polymaths of our time; the only thing he hasn't yet invented or excelled in is a sailing hovercraft. Only Ian Day has done that.

James has, quite incidentally, given us in the course of his story a fascinating history of speed-sailing from its earliest days; especially of the Portland meetings since their origin and with all their vicissitudes. Of course the history of Portland is inextricably woven in with *Icarus*' life story – one could never think of one without the other. So, added to the technical treasures of James's research we have here a chronicle of the whole new sport, a chronicle of the greatest value.

We can all welcome this book with relish, as the achievement of an intellectual athlete and a highly literate one. Any two of these qualities are rare enough in combination, but all three – well, words fail me!

Sir Reginald F. B. Bennett   1987

Preface

•

If only I was laid flat for a couple of months . . .

For five years or so I wanted to write an account of *Icarus*, but lack of time prevented me. Likely source material was kept filed away, and I talked occasionally with possible publishers. Then in late summer 1985 I slipped a disc in my lumbar spine, quickly losing sensation and power in my left leg. X-rays confirmed the diagnosis and I became an enthusiastic subject for an operation. Coming round from the anaesthetic was blissful. I was pain-free for the first time in months. This new-found tranquillity was shattered by the realisation that I was, in essence, 'laid flat for a couple of months'. A phone call home mobilised the appropriate files and papers. The first day and night (one does not sleep much in hospital) were spent by reading magazine articles written by myself, more than forty of them. This was not quite such an introspective experience as it sounds since they dated back over the years, and the early ones were unfamiliar. By the time I left hospital twelve days later the first draft was more than half written.

Although it required re-writing twice, the task was underway. Completion has been made easy by the various people listed below.

My thanks are due to *Icarus'* co-owners, who get ample mention in the story. They share all the credit for the success of *Icarus*, and none of the blame for this account which is mine alone. In writing it I have had constant support and encouragement from my wife Catherine, and all the family have put up with the reduction in what little time I had available for them. From the publishing side Phoebe Mason, then of Stanford Maritime, enthused at an early stage, and Peter Coles and Janet Murphy of Adlard Coles have given unwavering support and advice more recently. Divna Cox has coped with the work involved as an extra to her normal busy job as my secretary. Illegible scrawl and inaudible tape have become immaculate typescript at her hand, and she has become expert at word-processing. My profound thanks go to her for doing all this with such good humour.

Introduction

This book is about hydrofoils, and a working definition of the word 'hydrofoil' (synonym 'foil') is essential. A hydrofoil is a wing-like object attached under a water-borne craft. As the craft moves through the water a force called 'lift' acts at right angles to the flow, fulfilling the purpose of the foil in supporting or stabilising the craft. There is also a force called 'drag' which tends to slow down the craft and must be overcome by a source of energy such as engine, sail or human power. The ratio of lift to drag is thus a measure of the efficiency of a hydrofoil, and one important object in design is to make this ratio as high as possible. A typical drag curve for a hydrofoil craft, as shown overleaf, indicates the 'hump' in drag as speed increases before takeoff, followed by reduced drag thereafter making it relatively easy to sustain foilborne flight. The remarkable feature of a hydrofoil system, if properly designed, is that the drag increases only a little with a further increase of speed: such a craft has no top limit to its speed, at least up to 40 knots.

Hydrofoils may be compared with aeroplane wings, and in the previous paragraph the words 'aeroplane wing' and 'air' may be substituted for 'hydrofoil' and 'water'. The fundamental point of similarity between wing and hydrofoil is that each must be fully immersed to be effective. The aeroplane wing is always fully immersed in air, and the only effective part of a hydrofoil is that which is fully immersed in water. Hydrofoils and their supporting struts should thus aim to have minimum interference from the water surface. They should traverse the surface at steep angles, and the number of units piercing the surface should be as few as possible and as slender as possible. Spray and the formation of waves represent wasted energy, and good foil design keeps them to the minimum. The functioning parts of a foil system thus 'run deep' causing neither spray nor waves. This approach is the opposite of a planing hull, either motor or sail powered, which gains the necessary lift by contact with the water surface inevitably causing spray and waves. Nonetheless hydrofoils are impractical for everyday use on small craft, being both fragile and cumbersome, with some hazard to their users and others. Thus their best application is where speed itself is the main objective.

The centreboards and rudders of small sailing craft

Lift and drag forces on a foil section.

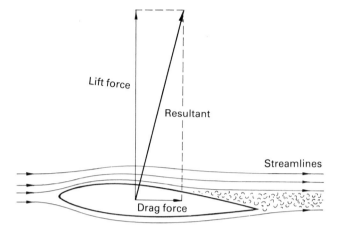

Typical drag curves with and without hydrofoils.

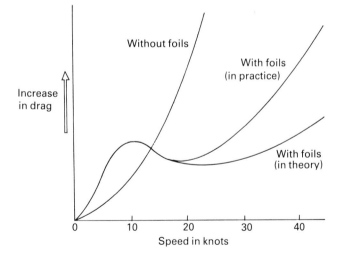

may or may not be included within the definition of hydrofoil. This wider definition involves lift acting in a horizontal direction, as is common practice in discussing the dynamics of aircraft fins and rudders. In sailing boats, centreboards and rudders are designed to produce maximum lift for minimum drag in a manner identical to that of lifting hydrofoils, and in fluid dynamic terms the wider definition is thus justified. In the racing dinghy world this similarity is recognised by the firms making centreboards and rudders referring to their products as foils.

The measurement of speed itself was responsible for the origin of 'speed sailing'. This has become a well established fringe activity in the world of sailing, with regular annual competitions in England and France, and numerous events in other countries on a less regular basis. Accurate measurement has provided proof of the phenomenal speeds reached by sailboards – 38 knots in 1986 – and of the ability of hydrofoils to greatly increase the top speed of a Tornado catamaran. The story of *Icarus*, the hydrofoil conversion of the Tornado, runs parallel to that of the sport of speed sailing. This book tells the story and also attempts to portray the pleasure and excitement that various other hydrofoil projects have given, and maybe it will lure a few people into trying for themselves. The appeal of a virtually unlimited top speed is best described in the words of American pioneer Don Nigg, more than twenty years ago: 'On many occasions the sail of the prototype was permitted to spill wind because of lack of courage on the part of the helmsman; the boat would have gone even faster.'

CHAPTER 1

A Wind Tunnel and a Tornado

•

Life is the art of drawing sufficient conclusions
from insufficient premises.
Samuel Butler

Oundle School excels in the production of science students. A strong tradition in science started early this century under the Headmastership of F.W. Sanderson and resulted in a set of workshops and laboratories far in advance of other schools. The workshops consisted of a forge, a foundry and a huge metal workshop as well as carpentry and wood shops. Each boy was granted one week off each term to go full-time and thus quite an elaborate project could be seen through to completion within the week. It also gave one a taste of 'artisan life', going off to work all week with his hands – in marked contrast to every other week of the term. I relished the workshop weeks and thrived there, perhaps aided by access in school holidays to a small workshop set up by my father; he is an Old Oundelian who just overlapped the time of Sanderson, and the home workshop is thereby explained. This acquisition of manual skills at home and school played its part years later, both in making hydrofoils and in choosing a surgical career.

The science laboratories were also well equipped, with ample apparatus for each boy to 'do it for himself'. However it was the calibre of teacher attracted by Oundle's reputation which was the greatest benefit. The basic principles of the scientific method were ingrained in the teaching of the natural sciences; time and again we evolved an experiment to test a hypothesis, and recorded our results and drew conclusions. This system produced a score of boys each year sitting four A Levels in science (zoology, botany, physics and chemistry). I opted for these pre-medical subjects as a matter of choice, although well aware that four generations of Grogonos had become doctors. The only exception in the family tree was, quaintly, any branch producing three sons; there the third son seemed destined to become an engineer. A great uncle, an uncle and a younger brother were all engineers, the only non-doctors in the family at the time I qualified. The A Level exams finished in June 1954 and the end of the summer term was still five weeks away. I was fortunate in having a small research project ready to occupy my time.

Science sixth-formers were required, either individually or in small groups, to prepare each year a 'conversazione'. It consisted of experiments or demonstrations of some aspect of science, and a high standard was expected. I had seen a small wind tun-

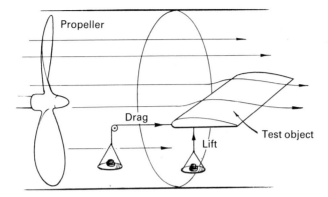

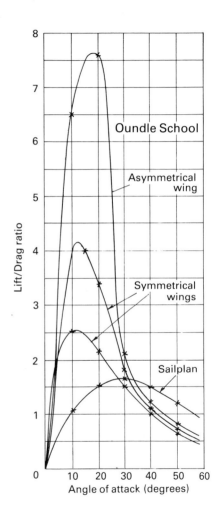

nel tucked away in a cupboard, at a time when the pressure of exams was on. It was a simple device with a 4 in diameter outlet and the necessary scales and balances to measure the lift and drag of any object placed in the airstream. I wished to compare sail rigs with aeroplane wings: it seemed to me that both were trying to do the same job, albeit positioned at right angles to each other, and I had an impression of severe inefficiency of the sailplan. I hoped to give numerical value to the difference, and maybe thereby proceed to put wing sails on sailing boats, models at first and full-size later.

The wind tunnel had been supplied with various small aeroplane wings of different sectional shapes, and I constructed model sail rigs of similar size. The aeroplane wing is several times more efficient than the sail in generating a high lift to drag ratio. Allowance must be made for the wing being smooth and professionally made, and the sail rigs rather crude, although I did my best. There are several other pitfalls, in aerodynamic terms, in transposing these results to a different size and different velocity. The conversazione went well, and I continued taking readings while visitors came and went since I needed all the results I could obtain in the time available.

I spent a further year at Oundle, attempting to improve my literacy since science had dominated the previous three years. Nonetheless the seed had been sown. It took some years to germinate, and then, strangely, grew downwards instead of upwards. I did not attempt to apply wings to sailing boats, but instead started ruminating about the inefficiencies of the underwater parts of boats. If a wing can do so much better than the normal sail rig above the water-line, what might not an underwater wing, or hydrofoil, do in replacing the paraphernalia of hull, keel and rudder?

The story now jumps four years, since medical student life at The London Hospital was a busy one and schoolboy experiments seemed remote and somewhat childish. In this gap I did a lot of dinghy sailing and became convinced that hydrofoils, if correctly applied, would increase sailing speeds considerably. There was no opportunity for research into hydrodynamic or hydrofoil theory, but I sketched out a likely design utilising a 'disposable hull' suspended beneath a frame on which were attached the mast, sails and hydrofoils. I was now confronted with a problem: I had known of no other attempts at sailing on hydrofoils, and was convinced that I was sitting on a winner. I therefore chose to show the designs to no-one except immediate family members and wait until such time as I might be able to put my ideas into practice.

The long periods as a student on midwifery attachment, waiting for something to happen, provided the time to set the design on paper, addressed to my engineering uncle. I have resisted the temptation to improve the text, but have left out irrelevances.

Dear Noel,   20th March, 1959
I heard you were going to have a talk with my father about boat design, and thought I would send you my scatterbrained idea.

The Objective: To make a machine which will go at very high speeds under sail in calmish water and a reasonable breeze.
1   The machine will be on hydrofoils.
2   At high speeds the apparent wind will always be well ahead of the beam, and much increased in strength.
3   If you are up on the foils the flotation hull is
    a)   so much dead weight
    b)   much extra windage.
b is a very large factor because of 2, therefore get rid of it (i.e. dispose of the boat hull).
The machine will then be in a state where it will sink if it comes off the foils, but
a)   it is much less likely to do this once the dead weight of the boat has gone.
b)   it will have a very good chance of getting through the eye of the wind on foils. The practical problem is merely that of getting rid of the boat.

Ideas on the Design: The machine will consist of a frame on which sails, hydrofoils and steering gear are attached, and from which a lightweight orthodox hull will be *suspended*, once on the foils. The orthodox hull can then be jettisoned. This is a very rough idea.

The Foils: I am quite convinced that for sailing

Original sketch of frame, rig and foils minus boat hull.

FAR RIGHT *Forward view showing hull suspended from frame after takeoff.*

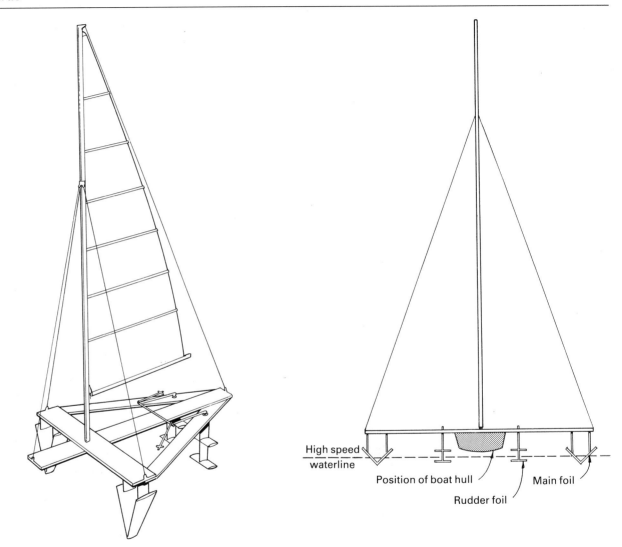

High speed
waterline

Position of boat hull

Main foil

Rudder foil

Main foil design.

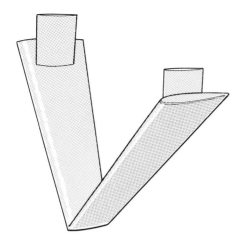

you must use Vee foils, with the usual hydrodynamic sections.

Advantages: i) Lateral resistance and vertical lift.
ii) Only the minimum amount of foil to support the boat's weight is in the water at any given moment.

Construction: Would have to be all metal, aluminium plating a rigid frame.
Sailing would depend on:
i) Steady wind never going outside the range 3–6 (Beaufort).
ii) Having calm water.
iii) Having a boat standing by.

Maximum Possible Speed: There is no theoretical reason why it should not go 40 knots.

I shall be glad to receive your condemnations, and have this letter back sometime.
Yours,
James

Noel had one or two discreet discussions with engineering friends, returning a reply that the idea was hopeless and would not work. So there it rested. The designs stayed safely stored away, representing, as far as I knew, a completely original idea. The next nine years were occupied by pursuit of a career in surgery, and a great deal of other sailing shared equally between racing and cruising.

Yachting World published the design of the Tornado in October 1967 (see pages 14–15). The prototype had been entered in the International Yacht Racing Union (IYRU) trials to select a two-man catamaran. The design provided a huge sailplan, a wide platform of a boat and an amazingly light total weight. The calculated power to weight ratio was found to be better than the fastest dinghies by a factor of two. Here was a perfect craft for hydrofoil conversion, fortuitously designed for another purpose. While the Tornado went on to win selection by the IYRU, I became restless now that the task was 'merely' that of designing and structuring hydrofoils. My funds, however, would not run to the purchase of a Tornado on my own, and I was not willing to borrow. I was also determined not to jeopardise my surgical training and career, having already taken a year off in an unsuccessful bid to go to the 1964 Olympics as singlehander in the sailing team.

There are three necessary ingredients in surgical training: first is acquisition of the Fellowship of the Royal College of Surgeons, second the publication of respectable surgical literature, and third appointment as a Senior Registrar. Although the last is not itself a guarantee of lifelong employment (that only comes with a Consultant post) it is likely that trainees who have passed all the other hurdles, with at least eight years of commitment to the specialty behind them, will not be left jobless at the end. I had passed the Primary Fellowship in 1964, and the final part in 1966. This released me into the arena of surgical publication, and I had several projects ready made for the printed word: a handful of articles soon appeared. The critical acquisition of the final training grade, the Senior Registrarship, came in 1968. The job itself was not unduly demanding and there was no question of applying for a Consultant post for several years. Had I been set on a career in 'academic surgery' in a teaching hospital then every spare moment would have been needed for ambitious research projects. However I had a hunch that my career would lie in serving a community, closer to the family origins in general practice. I did not want to be immured in an impersonal, albeit famous, big city hospital, where the patient is a 'fascinating case of Apfell-strudle Disease' instead of a '55 year old woodworker with a colonic growth' or some such. If there was to be a right time for a sailing research project then the years 1968–72 would surely be it. There was also a practical advantage in having a sailing project which could be pursued in my own spare time: dinghy racing would often be frustrated by the duty rota in the hospital, but it would always be ready waiting for any spare time I could find.

My reluctance to borrow or spend large sums of money was a matter of common sense. I had pursued a variety of other objectives in sailing, from cruising the Baltic to a large amount of dinghy sailing, especially team racing. None of these activities had involved risk money beyond the entry fee of a regatta. Although in 1968 I was actually losing sleep following the publication of the Tornado catamaran design, I was far removed from risking money on a hydrofoil project and so did not seek support from my immediate family, although I had shared in various sailing projects with my father and two brothers. Instead I teamed up with John James (photo inset), an exact contemporary at school who has been a lifelong friend. We chanced to row in the same crews throughout my rowing career. We often won, and for want of evidence to the contrary I believed that each contributed equally to our successes. However, I had some anxious moments, and my place in the First Eight was less secure than his. I never rowed seriously after leaving school, but John proceeded to row for University of London while they became all-conquering, and then for Tideway Scullers in a four which went through a nearly unbeaten season in 1964, and on to win a Silver Medal in the Tokyo Olympics. This led to a slightly painful review of my past rowing career: I had, throughout, been pulled along by one of the best oarsmen this country has ever produced.

In the ten years since leaving school John's life had been dominated by rowing and mine by sailing, and we only met on rare occasions. However he returned from a visit to Australia in 1968 and was instantly enthused by the hydrofoil project. We were, of course, risking our money in the purchase of a Tornado, but at worst we could sell the boat after one year and probably recover most of the cost. We knew in advance that the cost of materials for the foils would be small, although a large number of man-hours would be required for construction.

I spent many hours studying the theory of hydro-

John James.

foils. A friendly public librarian produced several tomes on fluid dynamics, and we had early advice and help from Alan Buckle of Lloyds Register of Yachts and Dr Alan Alexander of Loughborough University. The publications of the Amateur Yacht Research Society (AYRS) also helped, but were initially discouraging since it seemed that someone else had got there first. Under the editorship of Dr John Morwood the early AYRS journals were full of talk about sailing hydrofoils, and at least two projects, both in the USA, had already been successful in sustaining 'flight' above water. However there seemed to have been less success on this side of the Atlantic, and no-one claimed sustained flight. The nearest had been the father and son team of Ken and Terry Pearce,

Tornado hull showing foil strut passing up through centreboard case.

whose famous small catamaran *Endeavour* had been equipped with foils in 1966 and very nearly flew. Thus we were not deterred by 'prior art', and we gleaned every available scrap of information before starting to design our own foils.

The choice of hydrofoil options is bewildering, and the range of possible shapes, sizes, configurations and methods of construction seemed endless. Nonetheless the decisions had to be made. We opted to carry the main load of the Tornado on a pair of foils aft set at 40° under the boat, with a strut passing up through the centreboard case. This would make good use of the boat's own strong points, but later produced amazing practical difficulties in getting it in and out of the water. The front foils would be smaller and lighter, set quite near the bow, and also entering the water at 40°, with a vertical strut. No attempt was made to steer by means of the foils, and we simply planned extra long rudder blades for the Tornado's own rudder stocks and tillers. The size of the foils was dictated by takeoff speed, and Dr Alan Alexander produced a simple formula for 'practical hydrofoils' which proved accurate (see Appendix). Takeoff was planned to begin at a speed of 6 knots and be complete by 8 knots. The necessary foil area was 23 sq ft, two-thirds in the aft foil and one-third forward. Each foil had a strut supporting its lower part, and the foil tapered from the strut attachment downwards. At high speed the junction of foil and strut was intended to ride just above the water surface, the craft's weight being carried on the unsupported tips of the four foils.

Once the design had been finalised there was a real pleasure in constructing the foils. We took advice on the choice of wood from Brian Saffery-Cooper, who was a timber expert in addition to pipping me at the

Front foil, showing the primitive method of attachment.

post for the 1964 Olympic selection. The foils were laminated out of 3 in strips of Douglas fir and their shaping was an arduous but pleasant task. My father's workshop was invaluable, as was his ability to sharpen blunt planes. John James contributed huge amounts of time, a fair amount of it at night. He had given us a deadline necessitated by his long-term plans to return to Australia, which made us work hard, but an unforseen attraction sometimes kept us away. We had duly purchased a Tornado from Alan Bell of Whitstable, and it lay assembled at the Royal Corinthian Yacht Club in Burnham-on-Crouch where we took time off from the workshop to 'evaluate' the boat without foils. This was exhilarating, producing far higher speeds than we expected, and we realised that we were making the foils too large and could have opted for a higher takeoff speed, with considerable hydrodynamic advantage. Various family members and friends had now become enthused, and much help was given at critical moments. In early September of 1969 the foils were completed and taken down to Burnham on my father's trailer one Saturday morning. Family and friends helped to lift the Tornado onto high-level supports. The foils were fitted on by screwing through the plywood shell into prepared blocks inside the hull, which gave an impression of strength and rigidity when assembly was complete.

The problems of transporting the assembled craft to the water had not been thought out. The team could not manage it, and half a dozen unsuspecting passers-by were recruited. The whole contrivance was carried over the sea wall, shoulder high, and launched into deep water. The passers-by, especially those who unexpectedly got their feet wet, were thanked and rewarded as best we could with a nip

Icarus shoulder-high on the way to her first launch, August 1969.

Icarus' *first flight,
showing a
remarkable* lack *of
speed when
foilborne
singlehanded;
August 1969.*

of whisky. This first day was windless, but towing trials behind a motorboat suggested that takeoff would occur at about 10 knots, as planned. We were lucky not to break anything behind such a large and overpowered craft, since its wake and propeller wash put undue strain on the foils. On the Sunday the wind blew a steady 12 knots and *Icarus* took off. Control when not foilborne was sluggish, but once up she was stable, 'light on the controls' and entirely manoeuvrable. When sailing singlehanded there was a remarkable *lack* of speed: she seemed to heel before accelerating, and although foilborne in a light breeze estimated at 9 knots, there was no suggestion of improved performance as a result of the foils. However when two-up, with one on the trapeze, there were bursts of speed which seemed to justify the endeavour but without proof of increased speed. Alas, we had failed to make the external attachment chocks strong enough. They failed on two of the four outings that year, on the second occasion damaging one of the hulls. Nonetheless our object had been achieved, and John James set off for Australia taking with him much of the credit for the first hydrofoil 'flight' under sail outside the USA.

*Bursts of speed
when two up,
September 1969.*

Original Tornado design as published in Yachting World, *October 1967.*

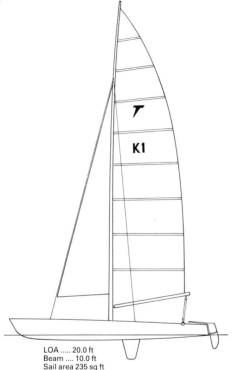

LOA ..... 20.0 ft
Beam .... 10.0 ft
Sail area 235 sq ft

Reprinted from **Yachting World** *October 1967*

Tornado

A B Class catamaran for international racing designed by Rodney March

TORNADO was designed with the requirements of the International Yacht Racing Union for a B Class catamaran well in mind, and to such good purpose that, following the trials at Sheppey in August, she is the boat that will be recommended to the I.Y.R.U. at its November meeting by the Observation Committee as a one-design class suitable for international racing. Rodney March set out to design a boat which would have an exceptional performance. This characteristic would necessarily stem partly from a light boat which in turn would make her easy to handle ashore. The third important factor is that Tornado is especially suitable for amateur construction, using the 'bent ply' method of forming the hulls.

Tornado's construction is the same as the bent ply method employed for *Thunder II*, which was a development of John Mazzotti's Manta construction. By presetting the keel angle when initially sewing and taping the keel together it is easily possible to maintain accurately a definite hull shape which can be repeated exactly. Three bulkheads and a piece of pre-shaped polystyrene foam for the forward stations assure perfect conformity to hull lines.

This method of construction lends itself well for amateur construction as only the minimum of jigging is required to hold the two 4·5 mm ply halves of each hull at the correct angle while the epoxy bonded glass tape sets. A further simple jig is made to give the correct deck level plan. This jig can simply be made from hardboard with a piece of 7/8 in square screwed around the hole pre-cut to accept the hull.

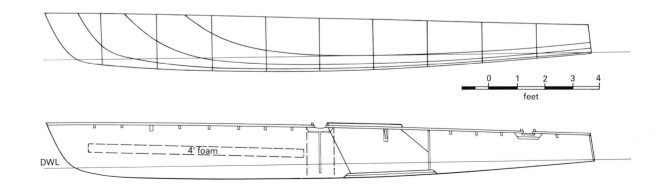

0   1   2   3   4
feet

4″ foam

DWL

The result is a hull with very soft lines which, in spite of the thin skin, is strong, rigid and very light.

The now familiar configuration of aluminium beams and Terylene 'trampoline' are used to tie the two hulls together and plug the hole between hulls. Four stainless steel straps on each hull hold down the beams which correctly align the hulls on assembly. The bolt ropes of the trampoline fit into aluminium extrusions screwed to the hulls and into the after beam, which is a mast section complete with luff groove.

Tornado promises to be a very popular boat; she is undoubtedly very exciting and for the first time brings in the added requirement of downwind tacking even in lighter winds, hitherto a waste of time with boats of her size except in special conditions.

CHAPTER 2

Evolution in Wooden Foils

•

In spite of all their friends could say
On a winter's morn, on a stormy day
In a Sieve they went to sea!
Edward Lear

Icarus' first season finished on a high note with technical success in becoming foilborne, some good action pictures in *Yachts and Yachting*, and the formation of a new syndicate consisting of Bernard Grogono, his three sons Alan, James and Andrew, and John Fowler. This group, with the addition of David Pelly two years later, has remained unchanged to the present day. Initial financing in November 1969 required £100 each, representing a one fifth share in the Tornado, and two years later a further £100 contribution from each to pay for metal hydrofoils. The syndicate members have shared equally in putting in their energy and ideas as well as finance. There is a 'timetable' of activity each year, starting in the autumn after each year's Speed Week. Modifications to *Icarus* result from discussions and exchange of letters, with an occasional round the table meeting of all owners if a major change is planned. Each contributes widely differing skills and attributes.

Andrew Grogono is a fully qualified engineer unlike the rest of the syndicate. He trained in the aeronautical industry and returned there in 1980 after ten years out. In earlier days he used his spare time to rebuild car engines, graduating from Cortina

Andrew Grogono.

to Aston Martin. At the time these were vital tasks, necessary to restore his only means of transport, in contrast to his later construction of the noisiest and most overpowered model motorboat ever seen. He also developed an inflatable sailboard which fitted into a suitcase for air travel, and went into production. He is a prankster and pyromaniac, possessing a cool nerve which has sometimes been necessary to quench his own 'successes'; his unmanned fireships have ranged well into the North Sea from launchings into the swift ebb tide at the mouth of the River Alde.

Andrew has been at the helm on five of the seven occasions when *Icarus* has made a world record. He championed the idea of widening the span of *Icarus'* front foils by moving them out sideways, and this has proved correct. He was the only syndicate member to understand the importance of going to France, winning the £4500 top prize in the first Brest Speed Week. He raised the B Class world record to 28·1 knots in October 1985 (see Appendix).

Alan Grogono is a Professor of Anaesthetics in New Orleans. He is also a raconteur, sharing with some comedians the ability to have his audience laughing well before he reaches the punchline of any

Alan Grogono.

Bernard Grogono.

John Fowler.

joke. He invented an anaesthetic machine which threatened a well-known product, and the company got the better of him by feigning interest as a means of suppressing it. He therefore took out a patent on his next invention, a simple anaesthetic safety device, and had to be bought out. He entered the computer field early and successfully wrote games programs against the professionals for a year or two. He has a great ability to organise those round him, and produced working parties of students to help run early speed trials for *Icarus*. Alan has spent 12 of the last 18 years in the USA and now contributes less to *Icarus*, but he often appears at short notice at Weymouth Speed Week. In 1980 he arrived by night in the middle of the Week, and set a new B Class world record of 23·8 knots within 12 hours of landing in this country.

Bernard Grogono carries some 'genetic' responsibility for the development of *Icarus* since in the 1930s he designed, but did not build, a stepped hydroplane sailing craft. Its essential feature was a 'gallery' running round the stern, enabling the crew to sit both aft and out when at speed. In the 1940s he designed and built a sliding-seat hard-chine dinghy; it looked like a slightly oversized Hornet but appeared five years earlier. His 9 ton sloop *Callegro* was used as 'committee boat' for the Burnham Speed Trials in 1970 and '71, on one occasion taking aboard 30 spectators which made her loll alarmingly.

John Fowler provides the necessary leavening among so many family members. He manages a farm in Essex, so close to London that suburbia lines every edge, and he utilises the main road that bisects his farm to sell 'bonzer' potatoes. He is an original thinker, contributing quite frequently to the correspondence columns of *The Times*. He has twice found fame by taking on 'big brother' singlehanded: once by conducting his own case against planning applications which would have ruined his farm; and once when he proved that a well-known stockbroking firm had illegally mishandled some of his funds, this second episode being taken up as a *cause célèbre* by the media. His early sailing included dinghy racing at Cambridge University where he was vice commodore, but in recent years he has spent more time cruising. Weymouth Speed Week often clashes with the potato harvest, and his son Johnathan has recently taken his place in *Icarus*, winning a new world record with Andrew Grogono in 1985.

David Pelly played a critical role, when not a syndicate member, in setting up the original Speed Trials in Burnham-on-Crouch. At that time he was assistant editor of *Yachting World*, and with editor Bernard Hayman he ran the Speed Trials which followed on *Icarus*' initial success in becoming foilborne. With the advent of sponsorship for Speed Week this role ended and David was recruited by the *Icarus* team. He has been a source of new ideas ever since, and has campaigned *Icarus* in Speed Weeks in Weymouth and Brest. In 1983 he wrote the book *Faster Faster*, tracing the history of attempts at speed under sail from the earliest times through to the present speed competitions. He is historian to the World Sailing Speed Record Committee, and yachting correspondent of the *Sunday Telegraph*.

The new syndicate wasted no time in redesigning *Icarus*' hydrofoils. We resolved not to go afloat again until they had been made fully retractable, to save the extreme difficulty of high-level launching. The structuring of new foils also provided the opportunity to reduce their size, thereby increasing takeoff speed and flying speed. In addition we opted to use

David Pelly.

Icarus' third set of foils, with front steering and a tip-over rear foil. (Photo Yachting World)

the front foils for steering, by mounting them on robust metal pintles instead of wooden attachment blocks. The 'tillers' necessarily faced backward, and were interconnected by the Tornado's own equipment. This new version was assembled hastily for the 1970 Earls Court Boat Show, just four months after *Icarus'* first flight. We teamed up with Alan Bell, builder of the original Tornado; he ran the Boat Show stand and sold Tornados, while we offered hydrofoils, somewhat half-heartedly, as a bolt-on extra. The Boat Show cost us nothing and produced no orders, but *Icarus* attracted a lot of publicity and we had a lot of fun showing her.

This second set of foils was a failure, since the bow foil was fabricated with an incorrect dihedral angle (the angle of entry into the water) and the area of

the main foil was too small. These defects were revealed in early season trials, when we had severe control problems and scarcely became foilborne. However, the new mechanisms did prove robust, and allowed *Icarus* to go afloat with all the foils stowed inboard. She could be sailed off from a lee shore into deep water, using the Tornado's own centreboards and rudders, and then converted for foil sailing. The main foils lay across the deck, mounted on a fore-and-aft tube outside the gunwale. They were deployed by tipping out over the side and locating up into the bottom of the centreboard box. A line passed up through the box to hold the foil in place, and the load was carried by beading which located on the edges of the box. The front foils were carried afloat resting on the trampoline and were then mounted on their pintles, which required calm water. There then followed a tricky manoeuvre: the boat's own tiller was disconnected from the Tornado rudders aft and carried forward to connect the rudder foils. Ample sea room was required during this manoeuvre since there were four rudders in the water, none of them under human control. Finally, the original Tornado rudders were unshipped from the transoms and carried on deck while foil sailing.

During that winter I had formed a Sailing Hydrofoil Group within AYRS, and with the help of *Yachting World* editorial staff the first speed trials were planned for May 1970. The third set of hydrofoils, vital for this meet, were thus constructed in some haste, still within a year of the start of the original project (see photo and Appendix). Their smaller size reduced construction time, and syndicate members turned out, often late at night, to ensure completion on time.

This first Speed Trial attracted a small entry of four foil craft and one standard Tornado. Speed was measured as the average of runs in opposite directions on an approximately 400 metre course set across the River Crouch. The fastest speed was Mike Day's standard Tornado *Galadriel* at 15 knots, in a wind speed of 12 to 15 knots. *Icarus* foundered early in the day, when the main foil strut seated in the wrong position alongside the centreboard box rather than within it, punctured a large hole in the hull. However, help was at hand, and within an hour of coming ashore the defect had been repaired. A plywood patch or tingle was formed to overlay the hole and secured with large amounts of tape. The following day *Icarus* successfully became foilborne, weaving through the anchorage in front of the Royal Corinthian Yacht Club for the benefit of spectators. The winds remained light and the unconverted Tornado was faster on the course. *Icarus* had several fast rides while off the course, and the syndicate was satisfied with her speed potential. The other two hydrofoil entrants, by David Chinnery and Joe Hood, showed originality but did not fly.

By this time *Icarus* had been developed through three sets of hydrofoils in less than a year. We had also run a stand at the Boat Show and an evening meeting in London covering all aspects of hydrofoil sailing. The syndicate opted to pause, since we could not justify putting further time and resources into a sport which no-one else wanted to play.

Our development had shown the need for smaller and stronger foils – the sort of strength that only metal could provide. However we decided not to pursue this idea until such time as a sponsor was found to run organised speed trials, for two reasons, firstly expense and secondly the lack of a defined objective. We were unable to organise accurate measurement

Icarus *at speed off the timed course, with the port hull repair in view.* (*Photo* Yachting World)

ourselves as well as getting maximum speed out of our craft. In addition there were no 'official' speeds to go for. We were up against claimed speeds, from either advertising material or journalists' reports which were unverified and often represented an optimistic guess. Speeds of 'well over 20 knots' were claimed for both the Hobie and the Tornado under

one or other of these headings. Our accurately measured speeds might, initially, be disappointing against such claims, and we would have no redress. However, if recognised speed trials were initiated, then such claims would either have to be substantiated or forgotten.

The conditions for speed sailing had been dis-

Alan Grogono at the helm and his wife Anthea on the mainsheet, at the moment of takeoff. (Photo Yachting World*)*

cussed at length in a *Yachting World* Forum held in Peter Scott's home in Slimbridge, Gloucestershire in 1970, and published in April of that year. They had also been tested afloat in the *Yachting World* Speed Trials in Burnham in 1970 and 1971. An informal organising committee met at the Royal Thames Yacht Club under Peter Scott's chairmanship, the members being Bernard Hayman, Don Robertson, Bee Mackinnon, John Fisk and myself. We agreed on the main conditions for speed records under sail, and decided not to meet again until such time as a sponsor could be found. Shortly after this meeting I resigned from the organising committee to maintain unequivocal status as a competitor, not an organiser.

This action prompted Sir Reginald Bennett MP, sometime later, to comment: 'You would not have got very far in politics; the only sort of committee you *never* resign from is one influencing events in your own sphere of interest'. This pause in development both of hydrofoils and organisation just happened to coincide with the appearance of Philip Hansford's small purpose-built hydrofoil *Mayfly*.

CHAPTER 3

Mayfly

•

Small is beautiful.
Anon

Philip Hansford designed and built the catamaran *Mayfly* largely as a solo effort, his parents and their workshop being the only source of assistance. The design benefited from his professional skills as an engineering draughtsman, and his aeromodelling skills were reflected in the meticulous perfection of the construction. *Mayfly* and *Icarus* have many features in common, but there was no communication between their originators until each was complete. There were, however, common sources of information, especially the design of Don Nigg's *Flying Fish* as published in the AYRS journal.

Mayfly's greatest asset is being purpose-built for foils. The two 15 ft hulls were built by the tortured plywood method, with no centreboard cases. Each weighed only 36 lb. Philip's careful craftsmanship made them totally airtight, requiring installation of a vent to stop bulging out on hot days and sucking in on cold. Philip opted to carry the main foils on the boat's own front crossbeam. This provides extreme strength of attachment and allows the foils to be rotated on a transverse axis, up in the air for going afloat and down once in deep water. The angle of attack is set by means of an adjustable strut. The foils were fabricated from mahogany and shaped to an arc of circle on the upper surface and flat underneath, the standard ogival shape favoured by most sailing hydrofoil designers.

Mayfly's original rear foils were transom-hung rudders with a strutted Veefoil on each, mounted on inverted pintles to carry the weight of the craft when foilborne. Strong elastic shockcord held the foils up onto the pintles. Philip thus deployed four foils 'one at each corner', in a manner similar to *Icarus*. However he opted to carry the main load forward, creating an aeroplane configuration, as opposed to the canard of *Icarus*. (A canard is a flying machine in air or water with the controlling element carried forward of the main wing.) The original *Mayfly* was made so small and light that she gave the appearance of a model made, almost grudgingly, just large enough to accept a human form. She can easily be carried to the water's edge by two men, and must then be paddled off into deep water before the foils are deployed.

While building the full size version Philip, the aeromodeller, also built a perfect working model of *Mayfly* which he took to the AYRS *Yachting World*

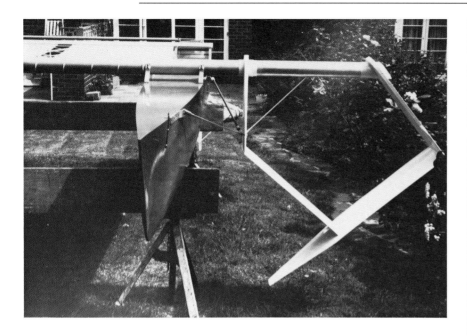

Mayfly assembled in the Hansfords' garden, showing her front foil mounted on the crossbeam. (Photo Philip Hansford)

The original rear foil, a complex strutted-V rudder foil, paired with another on the other hull. (Photo Philip Hansford)

Speed Trials at Burnham-on-Crouch in June 1970. He arrived late in the day and sailed the model in front of a small audience on the Royal Corinthian Yacht Club balcony. It sailed in a stable manner and at great speed, far outpacing the support boat. It was my misfortune to be in the bath at that time, recovering from an outing in *Icarus* where we had flown, but foundered: Philip had departed by the time I reappeared. He had mentioned, somewhat diffidently, that he was completing a full-sized version but would have difficulty in getting it to good sailing water. Happily someone had noted his surname and formed an impression that he lived in Greater London. I found him by phoning every Hansford in the London telephone directory, hitting lucky when halfway through the list of fourteen. We had several discussions on the phone, and arranged *Mayfly*'s first outing at Aldeburgh where the estuary waters provide perfect conditions similar to those at Burnham.

The following is my unedited account of sailing in *Mayfly*, written at the end of the first season.

Launching is easy, without trolley, as the boat is so light. Once afloat she must be paddled or towed into deep water, to put the foils down; this might present a problem launching off a lee shore with no outside help. Her sailing qualities, even in displacement mode, are adequate and she sails

Mayfly's first 'flight' was in June 1970 at Aldeburgh in Suffolk. During takeoff each rudder had five components traversing the water surface.

quite well on all points and will tack without going astern in calm water. The lift-out onto the foils is accompanied by an acceleration that would leave a sports car standing. It is easy to be overbalanced backwards from the sitting position if not forewarned. Once foilborne the boat has complete lateral stability, as would be expected by virtue of the very wide foil base and low-set sail plan. In the fore-and-aft axis there was initially a tendency for the bow to fall, but small outboard seats have been added allowing the helmsman to get well aft and the problem thus solved. Sailing on the foils is exhilarating, as always, but not difficult because of the boat's stability.

Tacking is accomplished by letting go the tiller and holding on! The stern, still airborne, travels rapidly across the water as the boat turns, and she comes off the foils almost stopped, but facing in the direction of the new tack. The tack takes a split-second, and requires no sternboard, but she carries no way round onto the new tack. However, the acceleration is sufficient to make up for this defect and I believe the time taken over tacking would compare favourably with any orthodox boat. She has not tacked fully foilborne, but gybed round on the foils on one occasion.

Fifteen years later one must question the wisdom of tacking by 'letting go the tiller and holding on'. It is one of the delights, and worries, of sailing small hydrofoils that the steering is unduly sensitive. *Mayfly* originally had no footstraps and one sat on the slippery, flat side deck and trampoline. A slight movement, produced by a foil passing through a wavelet, could start the helmsman sliding, tiller in hand. The slide was thus accelerated in an instant by the boat beginning to turn in the opposite direction. On one occasion at Burnham I was sailing two-up with Philip, he at the helm and I on the mainsheet. A small wave initiated a slide, and in a fraction of a second *Mayfly* had turned 180° downwind in her own length. Philip and I, obedient to Newton's First Law, continued our journey forward and fell into the water. *Mayfly* lay waiting upright and unperturbed about 12 ft away. The end of the mainsheet was still in my hand and we were soon back on board, but we could almost feel the reproach: 'More respect please, I am Formula One not heavy goods'. The thrill of sailing *Mayfly* never palled; she remained the easiest foil

Mayfly *at Burnham 1971, showing a reduction from ten to just one rudder unit traversing the water surface, and a hollow in the water in place of the hull.*

craft to get out of the water, the most stable once up, and gave the greatest impression of speed.

The symbiosis between *Icarus* and *Mayfly* was strong, and we formed a team with Philip before the first Weymouth Speed Week. We shared in commissioning metal foils for that week, Philip designing front foils which were smaller and stronger than the original ones but otherwise similar. He used the change to metal foils to produce a gross improvement at the rear end by converting to a single inverted T rudder, following on a successful experiment in this direction made in wood (see photo). *Mayfly* registered the initial A Class world record of 16·4 knots in the 1972 Speed Week. One of the *Icarus* syndicate always sailed *Mayfly* on the course as Philip was not keen, but the credit is entirely his, the sailing technique making little demand on the helmsman. Indeed the boat was sometimes sailed by individuals with no prior knowledge of hydrofoils, without untoward result.

Mayfly was entered for each of the first four Speed Weeks, gradually raising her A Class record to 21·1 knots. In these early years of speed sailing the only timed course available was in the centre of Portland Harbour, where the waves were between 1 and 2 ft high once the wind was up. *Mayfly*'s small size became a disadvantage since her foils would pass completely out of the water between one wave and the next, and splashdowns were frequent with occasional forward capsizes. In these conditions we would abandon the competition and sail to and fro close under the Chesil Bank at great speed and in complete isolation. One such venture has happily been preserved in the film *The Speedsailors* thanks to the producer John Walker (no connection with the whisky firm) sending a film crew and telephoto lens to cap-

David Pelly passing the central marker while setting a new A Class record of 21·1 knots in Mayfly. *(Photo* Yachting World*)*

ture it. In recent years this site has become the only one used in Speed Week, and now sees several hundred people gathered there, mostly watching sailboards chasing each other for the large sponsored prizes and commercial advantage of being the fastest in the world.

Philip remained uneasy about the limitations of surface piercing foils, and in 1975 built fully submerged inverted T foils with their angle of attack controlled by forward facing 'feelers' which ran along the water surface. The sensation of positive correction was immediately obvious, but the foils were unluckily overloaded by sailing two-up before they had been properly evaluated. Ten years later Philip completed a monohull version with surface sensors controlling the foils by means of trailing-edge flaps.

In 1976 I bought *Mayfly* from Philip for an embarrassingly small sum. However, the ownership of two hydrofoil catamarans proved difficult, and within a few months she passed on to Ben Wynne who was doing a thesis in hydrodynamics at Newcastle

Ben Wynne recorded Mayfly's *fastest ever speed: 23·0 knots in 1977, an A Class world record which stood for six years.*

One hull of Mayfly *seen end-on and showing the vertical tip added to the main foil; one of many ideas originated on* Mayfly *and copied by* Icarus.

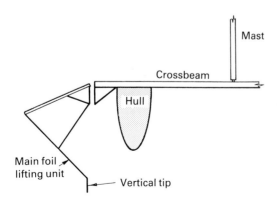

Seafly, *a robust imitation of* Mayfly, *was successfully campaigned by Terry Crompton in the late 1970s.*

SE DE VITESS

University. Ben completely redesigned and rerigged *Mayfly*. The front foils retained a roughly similar outline, but he introduced subtle changes in section shape towards the lower end. The foils were milled from a solid block by a computer-controlled programme which involved resources many times those used to construct the whole of the first *Mayfly*. Ben also introduced a vertically running tip at the lower end to reduce the amount of yaw, which had been limiting top speed as the boat's heading oscillated back and forth rather than holding steady. A new sailplan was also acquired and with Ben's enthusiasm the A Class record was raised to 23 knots in 1977. At that time this speed had only been exceeded in an official Speed Week by *Crossbow I* and *Crossbow II*. Ben continued to campaign *Mayfly*, but two windless years at Weymouth followed, and she suffered damage at Brest Speed Week in 1981. She did not sail again thereafter and now resides in the Science Museum in London, having retained her A Class world record until 1983, when it was taken by a tandem sailboard.

The story of *Mayfly* is incomplete without mention of *Seafly*, a semi-commercial version produced in Newcastle under the guidance of Colin Douglas. *Seafly* was a robust de-tuned catamaran, developed under the wing of the Training and Safety Co. of Swan Hunter Shipbuilders. Finance was found from a job creation scheme, and Terry Crompton, a well known dinghy sailor, campaigned one of the several Seaflies during the late 1970s. The 10 sq m sail area put her in a different class from *Mayfly*, and she recorded the fastest speed at one Weymouth Speed Week and also one Brest Speed Week, although neither speed was fast enough to take the record as it then stood. There was no market for the Seafly design, and the class has not been active in the 1980s.

CHAPTER 4

Weymouth Speed Week

•

If you want to win, choose a sport
no-one else wants to play;
better still invent *a sport,*
and keep it your own.
Author, in a lecture to the Royal Cornwall Yacht Club

In January 1972, at the London Boat Show, John Players announced their sponsorship of a World Sailing Speed Record competition. The prize money of £4000 would be equally divided between a September Speed Week at Weymouth, and an 'anywhere in the world' verified attempt. The Weymouth money would be further divided into £1000 first prize, and an equal distribution of the second £1000 between all competitors who came within 5 knots of the winner's speed. There were no rules about size of craft, sail area, crew number, wind strength, or angle to the wind; the craft was required to accelerate from rest under wind power alone, with at least one person on board, and be accurately and officially timed in one direction over a 500 m course. The RYA Organising Committee was chaired by Peter Scott, and the rules were evolved from those of the original unofficial committee which had agreed not to meet again in the absence of a sponsor. The only point of controversy concerned the 'one way only' condition. One group, myself among them, feared that this rule would evolve impractical craft, for example some sort of sled towed straight downwind by a parachute in a 60 knot hurricane. Peter Scott was forthright in opt-

ing for a one-way course, using a strange analogy with the Cresta Run and pointing out how slow would be the average of times going both directions in that event.

The *Icarus* syndicate had been waiting for the opportunity to design and commission metal foils for record attempts. A major effort went into this design process, with detailed help and advice from various individuals; Dr Alan Alexander had already provided theoretical information, and now answered further questions on foil characteristics and performance. We shared this knowledge with AYRS friends and rivals by running a meeting to hear his answers, in the same week as John Players announced their sponsorship. Don Nigg had replied by return to my initial enquiry about *Flying Fish* and we exchanged numerous letters. We were considering the use of metal foils with complex curved sections, like aeroplane wings. Nigg emphasised the view that simple arc-of-circle foil sections were adequate, and more sophisticated shapes a mixed blessing. First, it is impossible to obtain the very high lift/drag ratio from the book on aeroplane wing sections from small, practical surface piercing hydro-

End-on scale diagram of Icarus' *front foil, in use from 1972 until the present, showing 'Nigg-type' geometry. The force produced by the foil at takeoff (R_1) and at high speed (R_2) is shown.*

FAR RIGHT
Transom-hung inverted T rear foil with fences, summer 1972. The foil is mounted alongside standard rudder fittings.

foils. The lift/drag ratio for the aeroplane wing section is above 100 and for the arc-of-circle foil around 30, but the effective lift/drag ratio realised by the finished foil is about 10 whichever shape is used. There is thus a levelling down caused by such factors as surface proximity, ventilation, waves, and low aspect ratio. Secondly, it is desirable for the point on the foil which cuts the air/water interface to have a sharp leading edge to avoid unnecessary drag through throwing spray. Since the whole length of the foil, apart from the bottom few inches, passes in and out of waves in choppy water such as Portland Harbour, this effectively rules out any foil section with a rounded front edge. On the basis of these considerations we abandoned any attempt at using a complex section shape, and saved ourselves the large amount of time and difficulty that would have been involved in the attempt.

On an entirely separate topic, Nigg's analysis of stability factors led us away from incidence-controlled foils (i.e. with the foil angle altering to control flying height). He showed that excellent foil performance can be obtained with simple, fixed, surface-piercing foils each set at 45° dihedral angle. They can be made sophisticated in performance and response despite their simplicity, and can be designed with a large area and high aspect ratio when fully immersed, providing takeoff at a slow speed. Once foilborne the waterline travels down the foil with increasing speed, and there is never more in the water than the minimum necessary to keep the craft flying. A fully immersed wing or foil cannot do this, and the area has to be a compromise between slow speed and high speed flight. Commercial airliners try and improve efficiency over a range of speeds by using multiple flaps, and military aircraft

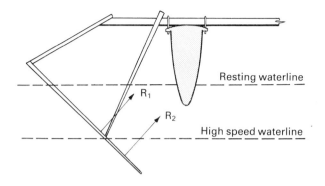

Resting waterline

High speed waterline

sometimes use swing wings, both of them attempting to solve this problem, but neither of these options would be practical for small hydrofoils. Nigg has also evolved the use of a single strut to support the foil, the junction being at the point which is planned as the high speed waterline. All the drag of the strut, inevitable at slow speeds, is thus lost as the highest speed band is approached. The foil tip then runs unsupported through the water surface at 45°, this angle being appropriate both to match the side force of the sail and to produce the necessary lift. Provided the water is calm and ventilation is avoided, it is likely that this foil produces a lift/drag ratio equal to that of a sophisticated wing shape running under water.

Nigg also contacted other American foil sailors and co-ordinated their replies. These exchanges between Dr Alan Alexander, Don Nigg and myself resulted in the book *Hydrofoil Sailing*, which the three of us co-authored. Mark Simmonds and Charles Barham helped us with expert advice. Mark was the hydrodynamicist of Southern Hydrofoils Co. and his practical experience in designing full-sized hydro-

foils was reassuring; he developed his own sailing hydrofoil at the same time. Charles Barham is a structural engineer and gave us specific advice about the tensile strength of various aluminium alloys, vital information for using the strongest possible materials to best effect.

In designing the new foils we used our experience with *Icarus* and *Mayfly*, and also adopted Philip Hansford's major modification of the rear foil. He had made an inverted T foil for *Mayfly*, the crosspiece on the T consisting of a symmetrical hydrofoil section set at 0°. It only produced lift in relation to the attitude of the whole craft. For *Mayfly* he had opted for a *single* central rudder foil halfway between the transoms of his catamaran hulls, with an ingenious 'false transom' which rotated to allow the rear foil to tip forward for going afloat. The *Icarus* team opted for double rudder foils, one hung on each transom. The new front foils are smaller than the final set of wooden ones, and the geometry is designed to take much of the lift force directly through their own mounting. The critical feature, for high speeds, is the junction of the main foil and its supporting strut. This junction rides just clear of the water surface at 25 knots, and the extreme strength of aluminium alloy is used to keep a reasonably high aspect ratio (i.e. ample length in relation to width) for the unsupported tip. At speeds above 25 knots there are only four components piercing the air/water interface, and at times this is reduced to three by keeping the windward foil just clear of the water.

The fabrication of the foils involved entering a field which was new to us. The starting point was a conviction that the strength must be situated in the two surfaces of the foil, since this is where the bending loads are carried. There is thus no advantage in casting foil units in solid metal since the core carries no bending load. Here we had some good fortune as an arc-of-circle section lends itself to fabrication in metal. A sheet of hard aluminium alloy is easily rolled to the appropriate radius; this provides not only the lifting surfaces of the foils, but two pieces could be welded together to provide symmetrical struts and the inverted T rudder foils. A further advantage lay in carrying the rolled sheet to the very edge of the foil front and back, thereby giving it extreme strength. The thickness/chord ratio changes inevitably as the foil tapers towards its tip; although the radius of curvature remains the same, and cannot easily be altered, the thickness/chord ratio gets less with decreasing chord, from 11% at the point of strut attachment to 6% at the tip. This feature is intended to delay cavitation at speeds around 35 knots, which would otherwise reduce performance.

Our close liaison with Philip Hansford enabled him to design a new set of foils for *Mayfly* using the same thickness and curvature of rolled aluminium sheet. He managed to incorporate his own design preferences, and we thus put together an order which was not labour-intensive. At this point I decided to try and fabricate the foils without expert help. Within the East End of London I found one firm to supply a sheet of hard aluminium alloy and another to roll

it to the appropriate radius. With a small power saw I undertook cutting out a section for *Icarus'* main foil, a noisy, risky, time-consuming job. At the time I was dating Catherine, and thought that 'holding the other end' was a reasonable way for her to spend an evening. I was quickly put right on this point, and we soon found a small advertisement for aluminium boat construction which led us to Bill Allday of Allday Aluminium in Gosport. Visiting him with my sample piece and various sketches proved invaluable, and in late January 1972 I sent him the details of complete sets of hydrofoils for three craft: *Icarus*, *Mayfly* and a late starter called *Hustler*, which would utilise similar foils to *Mayfly* under a different hull plan. We had failed to find a sponsor and I was reluctant to commit the syndicate to more than £100 each. Bill Allday and his fabricator John Simpson proceeded to make three sets of hydrofoils within our fixed price of £500, but I believed they subsidised the project. Allday found that full-welding (continuous lines of weld) distorted the foils, and might also reduce the strength provided by previous heat-treating of the metal. He therefore spot-welded each unit and filled the remaining gap with an epoxy-based paste. The foils were made exactly to specification, and we collected them in April. The photographs show how they were mounted on *Icarus*, and it can be seen that we copied Philip's successful transverse mounting system for the main foil. However we lacked the courage, initially, to mount the foils on the Tornado's own crossbeam and instead secured a robust beading outside the gunwale. This gave great strength to the foil mounting and also provided the scope to move the mounting position of the front foil fore and aft with ease. We opted to set it well forward, believing that more distance between supports would

Cross-section of lifting foil, showing simple construction with arc-of-circle upper surface, flat lower surface and giving great strength.

Curved plate

Spot weld and filler   Web   Flat plate

increase the craft's stability and reduce the risk of somersaulting over the front foil. We ignored the risk of instability caused by sharing the load equally between two sets of foils, instead of having one set heavily loaded and the other set for control, as in aircraft. This departure from orthodoxy prompted the remark that I would only fly in an aircraft designed by myself if it flew at a height of no more than 3 ft and a speed of no more than 40 mph above a 'soft' surface such as water.

Fitting the foils was easy, and the photo shows them as first fitted to *Icarus* at Burnham in May 1972. We failed to install fences on the first outing and found that air rushed down the whole length of the foil, with dramatic noise and an even more dramatic loss of lift. After a few minutes of uncontrolled

Bow view of foils showing the profile presented to the water flow. The strong wooden beading is foreshortened.

Icarus tuning up at Burnham-on-Crouch in June 1972.

porpoising we returned ashore and fitted fences in the usual way. These are small vanes perpendicular to the line of the foil, designed to prevent movement of air down from the water surface; they look similar to the fences on commercial aircraft wings, although those are used for a somewhat different purpose. Once fences had been fitted the control problem was largely overcome and we were aware straight away of a considerable increase in speed, as compared with the wooden foils. We made no attempt to measure our speed, since the RYA plans for the Weymouth Speed Week were going well and we anticipated that accurate speed measurement could be obtained for the cost of an entry fee. *Icarus* was the first boat entered for the first sponsored Speed Week.

The main feature of the first Weymouth Speed Week was novelty. The organisers were new to their task, and the timing and recording were initially very slow with long gaps between each attempt. Competitors were quite unprepared for the tough conditions caused by strong winds, even within Portland Harbour. The only craft performing well, without damage, were those *not* designed for speed sailing, such as Major Farrant's large trimaran *Trifle* and the standard Tornado cat, without foils, sailed by world champions Ian Fraser and Terry Pearce. The competitors' inexperience thus matched that of the organisers, and the few craft able to survive strong winds were able to make timed runs whenever they wished.

The sponsors failed to appreciate that Weymouth is not a wellfilled seaside resort in the month of October, and girls in frilly skirts met little success in trying to give away free cigarettes on the rainy windswept promenade. The old pleasure steamer *Weymouth Belle* moored on the course in Portland

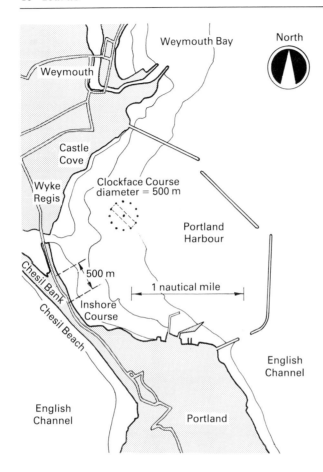

Plan to scale of Portland Harbour showing the original clockface course and the Inshore Course close to Chesil Bank.

Harbour was unused as a grandstand, although providing a welcome refuge for the few craft able to moor astern of her. Frilly girls with cigarettes had even less success than on the promenade, but the prepared food, uneaten by a non-existent public, was in part devoured by *Icarus*' spare crew; since the course was open all day crew swaps allowed for a large number of record attempts.

The timed course was set in the middle of Portland Harbour and consisted of a 'clockface' or ring of buoys set with great accuracy so that any corridor across the clock involved sailing 500 m. Although the harbour is sheltered on all sides by natural features or the harbour wall, its centre is half a mile from the nearest protection, allowing 2 ft waves to build up if the wind is strong. This gave an advantage to larger entrants, and several small craft with good potential were not able to show their paces. The Tornado came in the middle of the size range, faring better than the tiny craft and worse than the largest. Of the four large craft entered, only *Crossbow* was purpose-built. Her designer, Roderick Macalpine-Downie, had been asked by owner Tim Colman not to take risks in the design. Tim wanted to win, and made resources available for a boat of substantial size. *Crossbow* evolved as a one-way craft, able only to sail on starboard tack because of her asymmetry. Her 60 ft long, 2 ft wide hull carried a huge orthodox sailplan of 1000 sq ft and was held upright by the live weight of four or five men in a sidecar at the end of a spar 30 ft out to windward on the starboard side. She required a support boat to launch and recover, and at best could only make one run an hour. Nonetheless her sheer power and very narrow hull assured high speed. On the fourth day she had a spectacular mast failure which occurred in a gust with her crew 20 ft up in

Crossbow
*approaching the
timed section
during the 1972
Speed Week.*

Crossbow *on a timed run, in 1974–5, when a hydrofoil was used to reduce drag from the sidecar though not to lift the main hull.*

FAR RIGHT *Alan Grogono at the helm and the author on the wire during a timed run at the 1972 Speed Week.*

the air and led to their sudden and splashy return to the water surface. Despite this she went on to achieve 26·3 knots and won the £1000 first prize for Speed Week.

Icarus was the only other entry of reasonable size purpose-built for speed sailing. We benefited greatly from having opted for practicability; *Icarus* could launch in strong winds off the lee shore in front of Castle Cove Sailing Club and make her own way out through the moorings with all her foils inboard. Once in deep water the foils could be deployed, although with difficulty in 2 ft waves, and she was then capable of making one run every two minutes if the course was clear. We thus made a large number of timed runs and were able to experiment with different setting of the foils and sails, and different angles to the wind. We enjoyed the experience of spending most of our sailing time actually on the foils; the sensation and excitement generated by high speed did not pall and *Icarus* would often sail to and fro the full width of Portland Harbour whether or not timing was taking place. She was equally fast in either direction and would have benefited from a two-way competition in which speed was taken as the average of two runs in opposite directions. *Crossbow* would have been unable to run both ways, but a different rule would have produced a different design; it is likely that the same resources that produced *Crossbow* would have produced a high speed symmetrical catamaran of similar dimensions. This would have been a far more useful craft, capable of many more attempts each day, and might have gone as fast or faster than the one-way version.

Icarus was campaigned hard, often with two crew changes during each day, and she spent the week locked in battle with *Tango Papa*, an unconverted

Start of a 'Maypole' by the crew of a C Class cat.

Tornado. Ian Fraser and Terry Pearce knew that the Tornado's main problem, on a high speed reach, is burying the lee bow. They therefore devised a heavy weight slung to windward and behind the crew on the end of a pole, to counteract this. It is difficult to say how much the device helped, but *Tango Papa* simply would not reach 20 knots despite the expertise of her crew. *Icarus*, on the other hand, often leaped along at considerably greater speeds in a series of splashes and dashes. We found great difficulty in staying fully foilborne throughout the length of the course. On the third day David Pelly was helming, with Alan Grogono on the trapeze, and they entered the course at greater speed than ever before. *Icarus* had steering problems even in calm water, and the Portland Harbour waves magnified them. An 'acute steering problem' developed halfway down the course and *Icarus* achieved a manoeuvre identical to that once performed by *Mayfly*: she pivoted on the spot without actually capsizing. David Pelly was thrown into the water, but Alan, suspended on the trapeze, swung out on a circular grand tour which could well have become a Maypole if he had not brought the whole craft slowly over on top of him towards the end of his first circuit. Both boat and crew were undamaged, quickly righted, and competing again within the hour. Alan later admitted to some fear that he might have hit a solid part of the boat on his tour, but it is unlikely that anything solid, far less a foil, will lie in the track of a human body whatever the nature of the accident. In safety terms the only design feature which must be avoided is the positioning of trapezing crew immediately in front of a fast-running hydrofoil since a fall would probably cleave the person in two, especially since all surface piercing foil elements have knife-sharp front edges. *Icarus* finally achieved 21·6 knots thus resolving the hydrofoil issue by a clear 2 knots. An unconverted Tornado has never again appeared on Weymouth Speed Week.

Another element of the competition involved chasing the prize money. *Icarus* spent the first two days out of the money since *Crossbow* was more than 5 knots ahead. However, *Crossbow*'s broken mast allowed us to run on a particularly good day, and we crept within the necessary speed by just two-tenths of a knot. It was then *Icarus*' turn to suffer major damage, when a hull transom was torn off by the inappropriate force applied by her long, inverted T, rudder foils. Towards the end of the week both craft were ready for further action, but the wind had departed. The *Icarus* team spent the last weekend showing only a pretence of regret that the wind had gone, since we were the only craft within 5 knots of *Crossbow*'s speed. We thus departed with £1,000, an equal share of the booty.

Twenty other craft competed in Speed Week, but only two exceeded 16 knots; Major General Farrant's *Trifle* did 16·7 under reduced sail, and *Mayfly* reached 16·4. *Mayfly* was clearly capable of much greater speed, but her small size proved a grave disadvantage as the foils were so short that they would pass clear through a wave into the air: on re-entering the next one there was a risk of an air bubble remaining on the foil surface. This phenomenon of 'ventilation' is common to most surface piercing foils, which have fences to prevent it. However, they are of no value if the air finds another route to get there, as in *Mayfly*'s case. The air bubble may be washed off in less than a second, but this interval can be too long to avoid disaster and a splashdown. Such splashdowns do not often cause damage, since the slender catamaran hulls take the load quite efficiently, but they do eliminate any chance of that particular run being a fast one. Although no other craft achieved high speeds on the course that year, several were innovative in design and are described in Chapter Five.

Speed Week was over and *Icarus*' prize money reimbursed all those who had contributed towards the metal foils. However, a further £2000 seemed to be within our reach, the 'anywhere in the world' prize (the waves of Portland Harbour had prevented *Icarus* from ever putting together a single run at maximum speed). The driving force behind subsequent events was Alan Grog, whose job as Consultant Anaesthetist at the Royal Free Hospital now allowed a certain flexibility in taking time off midweek, and he also had access to students as helpers. We required an 'official observer' for each attempt and we were fortunate that John Fisk, Little America's Cup winner and Chairman of the IYRU Multihull Committee, lived half an hour's drive from Burnham-on-Crouch. Within three weeks of Speed Week we had established two accurately surveyed courses at right angles to each other in the River Crouch and the River Roach. This choice allowed us to run at a reasonable angle whatever the wind direction, and Alan set the pace in organising half a dozen more trials before the end of the year. A typical attempt would start on a normal working weekday with early morning awareness that the wind was up. I was living in a tiny tenement flat behind the London Hospital, six months wed to Catherine, and content for the *Icarus* team to rest on its laurels after a successful first year. The one tree in our tenement courtyard just happened to tap on our window in strong winds.

This would prompt a sleepy voice beside me to say, at about 7 a.m., 'I think Alan's about to phone'. This often proved correct, and a series of phone calls would follow while key members rearranged their day's schedules. An hour later various cars would set off towards Burnham for a further attempt to win the World Sailing Speed Record and £2000. John Fisk never let us down, turning out on every occasion as observer, and we made timed runs on five days, only stopping in the week before Christmas. Alan's students provided backup at the timing positions and we used my father's *Callegro* as committee boat. Our speed crept up to 25·4 knots, less than a knot from *Crossbow*'s speed, but there it stuck. We had faster bursts, but this grievance is common to all record attempts of any description: the fastest run of all never is the one that is timed. *Crossbow* thus gained a further £2000, and the *Icarus* crew took a rest.

CHAPTER 5

Innovators

•

The only way to get rid of a temptation
is to yield to it.
Oscar Wilde

The year 1972 was the turning point in the development of sailing hydrofoils; it saw the first speed sailing competition, and also the publication of the books *Hydrofoil Sailing* (Alexander, Grogono and Nigg) and *Sailing Hydrofoils* (AYRS authors). Up to that time most experimenters worked independently, although some were in contact through the AYRS meetings and journals of the 1960s, and for those in England I ran an AYRS Hydrofoil Group from 1969 to 1972. Research for *Hydrofoil Sailing* involved strenuous efforts to contact all individuals who had developed successful sailing hydrofoils. In this context success was indicated by sustained foilborne flight, in almost every case recorded by photographs. Although much might be learned from those who had tried and failed, it was difficult to unearth material for publication, and in fact the lessons learned by failure are available in ample measure from the early efforts of those who eventually succeeded. With the exception of Philip Hansford, all early sailing hydrofoil experimenters had plentiful experience of failure before achieving success.

From 1972 onwards the wide publicity given to speed sailing makes it unlikely that a sailing hydrofoil project would be developed in ignorance of prior work. The following account summarises projects before 1972, and describes subsequent ones which have been both innovative and successful. Further information on some designs is available from the Patent Office. Many of the patented designs have never been built, but all have one feature in common; the patentees felt justified in using time, trouble and expense in taking out a patent as a means of protecting their original ideas from exploitation by others.

The US Navy project, designer Mr J.G. Baker of Wisconsin, Illinois, remains as a standard for comparison with all subsequent craft. It was developed between 1950 and 1956, and involved money and resources many times those applied to any other project. *Monitor* was a complicated sailing machine, featuring an elaborate mechanical computer and linkage system which used forces on the rigging to control the angles of the foils in both the transverse and fore-and-aft axes. She was eventually timed at 30·4 knots, but there was no provision for verification by an outside observer. This speed is therefore no part of the official World Sailing Speed Records, which did not start until 1972. *Monitor* achieved less

Monitor *at speed —
about 30 knots, but
not timed officially.*

accurate measurements close to 40 knots, and a remarkable 15 minute film has recently come into my hands, giving credibility to her high sailing speed, but without any possibility of measurement. No other claim for a sailing hydrofoil is in the same range of speed. It is a matter of conjecture whether or not *Monitor* would have exceeded 38 knots in the conditions laid down by the WSSR Committee, and thereby be the present holder of the World Sailing Speed Record.

The next phase of sailing hydrofoil development involves two innovators in the USA, each pursuing almost identical projects during the 1960s while unaware of the work of the other. The best documented of these is Don Nigg, whose analysis of stability factors has proved invaluable in the design of many subsequent craft. Nigg's craft is of canard configuration, with two steeply angled, widely separated foils supporting the rear of the craft and carrying most of its weight. A lightly loaded steering foil at the bow controls both height and direction. Nigg evolved his ideas by trial and error over several years, and eventually responded to a request from the AYRS to publish designs of the fully evolved form *Flying Fish*. He sold about two dozen sets of plans, but doubts whether more than a handful of craft were built to his design. One was completed on the Isle of Wight by Captain J.C. Cockburn with some modifications from Nigg's plans, and flew successfully in Bembridge Harbour and in the Solent on a number of occasions.

The other American innovator in this period was W.S. Bradfield, Professor of Mechanical Engineering at New York University, who enlisted a series of student groups in a gradually evolving sailing hydrofoil throughout the 1960s and 70s. The choice of con-

Nigg's Flying Fish, *forerunner of many subsequent sailing hydrofoil designs.*

Flying Fish *foils set up ashore, showing the main foil at 45° supported by a strut, with a tapering unsupported tip: a feature copied by* Icarus *and many others.*

figuration was almost identical to Nigg's, although without knowledge of his work, and the project initially started with three floating 'pontoons' at the positions of the foils, but moved to have a single central hull and crossbeam with considerable improvement. Brad became a close friend of the *Icarus* team by coming to the first three Weymouth Speed Weeks. We picked his brains on matters of theory, and in return our practical experience, at that time ahead of his, may have helped a little with his projects. The 1975 version consisted of a single central Tornado hull and standard rig, the canard foil configuration providing stable flight. At this stage no accurate measurements of speed were made.

Prof. Bradfield and his students embarked on a

Professor Bradfield's evolving design of nf², *the 1975 version with a single Tornado hull.*

nf² *tuning up with a C Class rig in 1978.*

fully purpose-built sailing hydrofoil in the years 1975–7 and gave it the name nf^2 as an abbreviation for 'neither fish nor fowl'. The layout was similar to their previous version, and nf^2 was successful in achieving high speeds. Brad and his students set up a measured course within the criteria laid down by the World Sailing Speed Record committee, and successfully captured *Icarus'* world record in 1978 with a speed of 23·0 knots. They then came ashore to change to a larger rig and then went out to take the C Class world record with a speed of 24·4 knots. At this time Brad had the advantage of running a large engineering department in Stony Brook, Long Island and I visited him there in 1979. He had a huge barn-like shop in which nf^2 was fully assembled including rig and hydrofoils. At that stage Brad felt there was no justification for further record attempts with nf^2. Shortly thereafter he moved to a new post in Florida, and a new design is slowly evolving there in a similar manner to his previous ones.

David Keiper's *Williwaw* is the only successful sailing hydrofoil capable of cruising in open water, providing accommodation for a crew of two. The hydrofoil configuration looks complicated, but is effective. There are four foils, one at each end of a narrow high-sided 31 ft hull, and one on each outrigger of a trimaran configuration. The foils are built as 'ladders' as a means of gaining sufficient area from the available foil material, which was an 8 in chord aluminium extrusion. (The advantages of using an extrusion are described in the next chapter.) *Williwaw* sails on three of her four foils, the one on the windward float being clear of the water once she is up. All the foils are retractable by tipping over onto the deck. After prolonged trials in 1968–9 off Sausalito, Keiper sailed *Williwaw* across the Pacific

without difficulty. She has also sailed foilborne with nine people on board, more than twice the number of any other sailing hydrofoil. Keiper tried to popularise sailing hydrofoils at a much smaller scale by selling conversion kits for Hobie catamarans. He acquired lengths of 2 in chord extrusions, one a lifting section and one symmetrical, which were fashioned into a ladder arrangement similar in plan form to *Williwaw*'s foils. The Hobie conversion was not successful, producing severe 'porpoising', perhaps because the foils lacked fences and thereby suffered from ventilation. Short lengths of these extrusions came to England via the AYRS and were used as the front foil and struts of my sculling hydrofoil.

Bill Prior of Chagrin Falls, Ohio was remarkably successful in producing a sailing hydrofoil from the simplest components. He started with a Sailfish but his first effort was prone to 'do a slow roll over frontwards, which wasn't too desirable', and he devised a purpose-built framework of an 'aeroplane' configuration, almost identical to that subsequently used by *Mayfly* and *Icarus*. The photograph shows the front foils at 45° dihedral, with a single central rudder foil aft. Prior made an unsuccessful attempt at commercial application, and has not been active in sailing hydrofoils in the last 20 years.

The final group of hydrofoil sailors active before 1972 consists of three projects all using a catamaran configuration for hydrofoil conversion. *Icarus* and *Mayfly* have been described, but the third craft antedates both and was developed at the University of Michigan in 1966. Howard Apollonio built *Flying Feline*, a crude robust 15 ft catamaran, during one long weekend and applied himself to its conversion for hydrofoils. The similarities to one of the earlier configurations of *Icarus* are remarkable, but Apol-

LEFT Williwaw *at speed on San Francisco Bay in July 1969.*

Bill Prior's simple but successful hydrofoil.

lonio's work was only unearthed by Prof. Bradfield well after *Icarus'* development, and the *Icarus* team had no knowledge of his project. Apollonio's foils were fashioned in wood sheathed in fibreglass, and the junctions gave trouble by delamination and cracking. Trials in the open sea were carried out off the coast of Maine in 4 ft waves, and Apollonio was impressed by the boat's stability in wave encounter.

Leif Smitt is a Danish naval architect who has produced a variety of small hydrofoil projects over the years. He was initially a catamaran sailor and he designed and built a C Class catamaran which won the Little America's Cup from England, at second attempt, in 1968. The rules of the LAC specifically allow hydrofoils, but in Leif's opinion the difficulties of making an all-rounder for a triangular course competition are too great for hydrofoil application. Leif designed and built *Kotaha* for the first Weymouth Speed Week in 1972. She was a proa, reversing her direction of travel when tacking with the main hull always carried to leeward of the outrigger. The single sail of 10 sq m is set on a mast mounted on a sliding track, necessary to preserve the position of the centre of effort when reversing direction. There were three hydrofoils; at each end of the main hull were identical units consisting of a 45° dihedral arc-of-circle foil made of solid aluminium, obliquely attached to a vertical rudder unit. The foils are set at zero angle of attack to the water flow, and whichever one is the 'front' is locked in a central position, the unit at the back end being released for steering. The helmsman gives the foils a positive angle of attack by moving his weight well aft on a trapeze. The outrigger is supported by a small inverted T foil. Both hull and outrigger were constructed from polystyrene foam sandwiched in glassfibre and epoxy resin. This method of construction was ahead of its time, though it became popular for sailboard construction ten years later and was used by the author in making the high speed board *Dots*. *Kotaha* thus incorporated a handful of features never tried before, and her sailing qualities were excellent. Unluckily her hydrofoils were so small that she suffered similar problems to *Mayfly* in the open water at the centre of Portland Harbour, and her maximum measured speed of 13·6 knots was far below her true potential. She was damaged shortly thereafter and has not sailed again.

Leif Smitt's other hydrofoil projects, both in the

Kotaha *on a timed run at Portland Speed Week in 1972.*

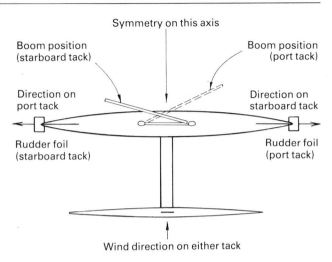

Symmetry on this axis

Boom position (starboard tack)

Boom position (port tack)

Direction on port tack

Direction on starboard tack

Rudder foil (starboard tack)

Rudder foil (port tack)

Wind direction on either tack

TOP RIGHT *Proa configuration, showing the symmetry of each end on a transverse axis.*

early 1980s, have been a human powered 'hopping hydrofoil', and his *Ugly Duckling* which is an uncompromising speed design utilising a Tornado rig on an asymmetrical proa. High speeds are only possible on starboard tack and the craft passes through a series of modes as speed increases. Initial displacement sailing is followed by the bow lifting quite abruptly onto its foil at 8 knots. The main hull then drags somewhat in half-displacement mode, but as speed increases to 13 knots it starts planing on its transom. The small rear foil built onto the rudder finally lifts the transom. The craft still has a slight bow-up trim, but with a further increase in speed she again becomes level. The surface skimming front foil sets the rear foil at its optimum position at the design speed of 34 knots. The outrigger has a small inverted T foil, but the helmsman will normally balance the outrigger and its foil just above the water surface by adjusting the mainsheet.

Leif Smitt's Ugly Duckling *sailing off Copenhagen.*

Centaurus II *with*
A Class rig,
recording 27 knots
in 1982.

Leif campaigned *Ugly Duckling* in 1983 in the Swedish Speed Week at Karlskrona, and later that year at Portland. Her speed potential was without doubt, but her uncompromising design posed problems in the context of modern speed events. She requires a lot of time for each run, greatly reducing the number of attempts she can make in a day, whereas the sailboards run repeatedly, accepting that some runs will not be timed on a crowded course. Leif believes that his best run at Portland that year was more than 30 knots, but was not timed. He has not yet found the opportunity to repeat it.

By remarkable coincidence a Russian sailing hydrofoil very similar to *Ugly Duckling* was developed at about the same time. There was no exchange of information between Leif Smitt and Aldis Eglajs, whose highly successful design has apparently evolved without reference to previous hydrofoils. The Russian *Centaurus II* carries the main load forward on a single inclined foil, with a small rudder foil aft. The outrigger is supported by another inclined foil, and the rig is boldly canted to windward. *Centaurus II* reached 27·0 knots with an A Class rig, which would have been a class world record if an officially appointed observer had been present. The author was granted this role by the WSSR Committee and corresponded with the Russian team in 1983, but the arrangements proved too difficult. The superficial similarity between *Ugly Duckling* and *Centaurus II* is more remarkable as the Latvian coast lies less than 200 miles across the southern Baltic Sea from Karlskrona. Despite this proximity each team worked without knowledge of the other, and it is disappointing that the two craft have never sailed against each other.

Only one person has successfully converted a stan-

dard racing dinghy to hydrofoils. Frenchman Claude Tisserand's initial craft was a purpose-built trimaran of around 16 ft, with a large foil area of 2·5 sq m, the foils being set at 20° dihedral and 8° angle of attack. In correspondence with the author a reduction of foil size and angle of attack was suggested, and also an increase in the dihedral angle to 45°. M. Tisserand also changed to a standard 470 one-design dinghy. The result was a practical boat with retractable foils which was timed unofficially at 20 knots. In 1974 and 1975 M. Tisserand came to Portland Speed Week, but the wave height on the offshore course prevented him recording a similar speed in front of official observers. He was intent on improving the performance of a 470 around a triangular racing course, and in this he failed. However, he increased the top speed ever achieved by such a dinghy by about 5 knots, and no-one else has been successful in this type of project either before or since.

Up to this point in the story all the successful craft except *Monitor* have used fixed hydrofoils. While sailing there are no moving parts except the steering mechanism. This emphasis on simplicity is appropriate for amateur design and construction especially since the cunning use of surface piercing foils can

Philip Hansford's Philfly, *showing Hook's surface sensor mechanism and linkage to control lift from foils. (Photo Roger Lean-Vercoe)*

produce stable and efficient flight over a range of conditions. However, such foils are vulnerable to increasing wave height, the rapidly varying immersion of a lifting unit producing a rapidly varying lift force: this always gives a bumpy ride in waves and encourages ventilation, sometimes with disastrous results. Incidence control of the foils allows more stable flight.

Christopher Hook, working in England and then the USA, was the pioneer of the 'surface sensor' mechanism whereby a light lever arm and float run along the water surface and control the angle of a fully submerged foil by a direct mechanical linkage. Hook's original work was with powered hydrofoils and included a US Navy contract, but his attempts at sailing conversion were less successful. The two

Force 8, *the Pattison brothers' incidence-controlled craft, has tacked without coming off the foils.*

craft which have proved the suitability of incidence control for sailing hydrofoils are *Force 8* and *Philfly*. *Force 8* was developed over a period of seven years in the late 1970s by the Pattison brothers, using their professional skills as naval architects. Their objective was to take the Open Class World Sailing Speed Record which then stood at 30 knots. The craft was small, built with no outside sponsorship, and the overall size of each component limited to that of the domestic garage where they were constructed. The problems of wave encounter in Portland Harbour led the Pattisons to choose vertical struts piercing the water surface, and the Hook Hydrofin system whereby all of the inverted T foil alters its angle in response to the surface sensor. The foils are capable of exerting negative lift as well as positive, and the

design allowed, at high speed, for the windward float
to be held down by its foil, while the leeward one
carried the load of the craft and the excess load from
the windward foil. The helmsman's control of the
foils was similar to that on an aircraft, with a wheel
that rotated to give roll input, and sliding fore-and-
aft movement to change flying height. The mechanism acted as an override to the surface sensors and
was quite complex. The stern foil was an inverted T
rudder foil, fixed at an angle of incidence of $-2°$ from
horizontal. The rig was a symmetrical aerofoil,
designed to withstand very high apparent winds
without distortion, and accepting the penalty of poor
performance in light airs.

Force 8 was awkward to get afloat. She was assembled at the water's edge with the foils and their mech-

anisms hinged up. The wing sail had to be tended at all times to prevent it taking charge. The boat was then carried into the sea by three tall men, and held while the foils were positioned and checked. At low speed the incidence control mechanism could be overcome by the side force of the sail, and care was required in gathering way. However, once speed picked up, *Force 8* sailed reasonably well in displacement mode, and once foilborne she became extremely stable. She required 12 to 15 knots of true wind for takeoff, and once foilborne showed exceptional stability. On the foils she was highly manoeuvrable, and once in 1979 succeeded in tacking rapidly through the eye of the wind without coming down off them. No-one else has laid a claim to achieving this manoeuvre, and *Force 8* fulfilled most of her objectives although failing to reach her maximum design speed. Her team planned minor modifications to improve performance, but she has not been seen on the water since 1982.

Philfly is the brainchild of Philip Hansford, of *Mayfly* fame (Chapter 3). In the 1980s he spent several years developing his own version of an incidence control hydrofoil, its general layout being similar to *Force 8*'s. However Philip opted for rear-facing surface sensors, and for the control to be provided by flaps on the fully submerged foils rather than the whole foil pivoting. This uses the control force more efficiently, and allows lighter linkage units and a smaller float. The main hull was a standard AYRS hull, and the rig was a well designed 10 sq m una rig (mainsail only) acquired secondhand. Philip's design also provides for the windward foil to produce negative lift if required, but the mechanism is far simpler than on *Force 8*; there is no override of the foil angles, and flying height is set exactly by the surface sensors.

Each part of the linkage system can be adjusted between one outing and the next, but *Philfly* proved stable on her first outing. I had signed on as Philip's pilot, but missed her first successful flight in 1985 following a slipped disc operation. In early 1987 she has yet to make a speed run, and the A Class record, standing at 34 knots by a tandem sailboard, may have moved out of reach.

A detailed account of innovation in sails and rig is outside the scope of an account of hydrofoil innovation. Nonetheless the interaction of rig and foils is considerable, and in three major areas. These are the use of kite rigs, the use of solid wing sails and the use of inclined rigs.

Kite propulsion has been pursued successfully by *Jacob's Ladder* and this team has also been involved with hydrofoils. Contrary to popular belief, the stack of kites is not used to provide lift since they are flown in a series of wide arcs fairly low down over the water. The power produced is much increased by 'sweeping the sky' in this way, energy thereby being extracted from a much wider corridor of passing air than if they are held stationary at the maximum height. The kites are 'rested' by letting them fly up into a stationary position at a high angle, which produces least power. The particular advantage of the kite rig in hydrofoil application is that the takeoff point on the boat is at deck level. There is thus almost no heeling force and the overall beam can be much reduced in comparison with *Icarus*. The main problem with kites is in setting and controlling them. The *Jacob's Ladder* team may make it seem a simple and practical exercise, but they now benefit from ten years experience, with a fair measure of disaster and difficulty on the way.

Solid wing sail rigs have a special part to play in

Jacob's Ladder *used kites on a Tornado to set the current world C Class record of 25·0 knots in 1982. A subsequent version, using hydrofoils of unusual design, has been less successful.*

relation to hydrofoils, since they generate in air the same sort of high efficiency that hydrofoils generate in water. In practice the lift/drag ratio of an efficient wing rig is much greater than that of a 'practical' hydrofoil, mainly because the foil suffers from its proximity to the air/water interface. A combination of high efficiency in the air and in the water would provide a craft that did not require a high true wind speed to achieve record speeds. The reason why solid wing rigs have not been more in evidence again concerns practicability: they are expensive, heavy and fragile, and particularly difficult to handle in high winds. Recent development of wings which are all solid has been mainly in C Class catamarans, and any

Gamma *uses an inclined rig that holds itself up while sailing.*

innovator venturing into this field would do best to imitate their 'state of the art'.

The third area of innovation concerns inclined rigs. They are a dubious advantage, despite taking some of the load off the foils. The reason lies in lessened control. Foil systems often lack control by having insufficient grip on the water, and a strong lifting force will increase this tendency. Nonetheless several innovators have made inclined rigs a major part of their foilcraft, including Didier Costes in *Exoplane*, and more recently *Gamma* and *Alien*. All show that inclined rigs can be made a reasonably practical proposition.

In addition to the innovators, there have been, from *Icarus'* viewpoint, a variety of 'imitators'. Most have tried to improve on her foil designs, and we have always discussed 'improvements' if asked. Nonetheless there was a fairly thorough research and development process (Chapter 2) before *Icarus'* metal foils were built, and as yet all changes attempted by imitators have been unsuccessful. This has led, in recent years, to successors being more and more like *Icarus* herself. In 1984 she was one of three identical Tornados with identical foils ranged side by side on the beach at Portland. Both the other designers, Alan Chilvers and Jean Bernard Cunin, are close friends of the *Icarus* team and they keep us on our mettle.

CHAPTER 6

Man-powered Hydrofoils
•
Nothing great was ever achieved without enthusiasm.
Emerson

The motive for this activity must first be established. Why should anyone wish to abandon the displacement principle for man-powered transport on water, and attempt to travel along supported only by the dynamic lift derived from hydrofoils? In simple terms, why does anyone want to fly rather than float? The answer lies in the quest for speed, coupled, in my case, with a loophole found in the regulations of the Amateur Rowing Association. My enquiry of the ARA in 1975 revealed that there was only one rule for single sculling craft as used in the Diamond Sculls at Henley Royal Regatta; a rubber ball of not less than 5 cm diameter must be fixed on the bow. (This is a safety measure designed to prevent spearing; a risk made more likely by the sculler facing backwards, and being reluctant to glance over his shoulder to see where he is going since the delicate balance is upset each time he does.) All other features of the craft were unrestricted and hydrofoils were not prohibited. My confidence in hydrofoils, based on success with *Icarus*, was such that the Diamond Sculls seemed to be within my grasp. Before describing the sculling hydrofoil, however, we must make some comparisons with flight in air.

Man-powered flight in air has aroused interest since antiquity. The lure was that of finding three-dimensional freedom, of 'joining the birds of the air and soaring towards the heavens'. This lure has been largely fulfilled, without relevence to man-powered flight, by gliding, hang-gliding and ballooning. For those not averse to engines, powered aircraft can also swoop about the sky with even greater freedom. Man-powered aircraft have evolved much more slowly and painfully, with several failures to accompany each technical advance. It has proved very difficult, using the limited horsepower available, to fly without the assistance of air currents, hill slopes or balloons. Stimulus to development was provided in 1959 by the Kremer Prizes, the first given for a figure-of-eight course round posts half a mile apart, and the second for crossing the English Channel. An account of the aircraft which won these prizes is given in the book *Gossamer Odyssey*. They are a far cry from swooping and soaring towards the heavens. It transpired that slow, low level, straight-line flight in still air is just possible with the modest power available; corners present formidable problems. It is doubtful if the Kremer objectives would ever have been reached

hydrofoil are features related to the far greater density of water when compared with air. The lifting units are tiny by comparison, hydrofoils therefore being easier to construct and far lighter than corresponding aeroplane wings. Problems of stability are also similar, especially for slow, low level, straight-line flight. For hydrofoils the crunch comes with the word 'slow': large foils would allow flight over water at very slow speeds, but there would be no worthwhile objective. Man-powered hydrofoils require a target speed so that the foils can be made optimum size. There is not sufficient spare power to make the foils ample in size, as can be done in sailing, and then test to see what speed can be reached. The target speed for my project was provided by Henley Regatta: the Diamond Sculls would be won by a speed just under 11 mph (4·92 m/sec). Since man-powered aircraft at that time flew at about 15 mph (6·70 m/sec) the power required would be only 73% of that required in air, if other factors were equal. Also, the empty weight of the sculling boat with foils and oars would be around 50 lbs (22·7 kg) in comparison to the man-powered aircraft empty weight of around 100 lb (45·4 kg) at that time. Add a 70 kg man to each and the laden weight of the watercraft is only 80% of the aircraft. The required power is thus further reduced to 65% of that required to fly in air. If this margin proved sufficient to offset the differences in training and technique between myself and the top sculler, then I would enter for Henley; if not then a specialist sculler would be encouraged to take over.

Design and construction of the sculling hydrofoil required only a small allocation of time and resources, occupying three weekends in April 1975. All the components were already in stock. The sculling boat had been acquired a year before on moving

without the incentives of £50,000 and £100,000 prizes for the figure-of-eight and Channel crossing respectively. The main advance made by the winning aircraft against their predecessors was their ability to fly very slowly, since the required power is directly proportional to speed.

Man-powered hydrofoils have a remarkable similarity to man-powered aircraft. The fluid dynamics are comparable, and similar design features are necessary to produce maximum lift/drag ratio from a hydrofoil or an aeroplane wing. In favour of the

to live close to the Thames. It was no coincidence that the boat, supposedly purchased for recreational use, was made of aluminium, allowing hydrofoils to be bolted on and off quickly. The hydrofoils were surplus to requirements for sailing projects and consisted of lengths of aluminium extrusion, of 10 cm and 5 cm chord. Both had the same cross-section profile shape, designated NACA 4412, which allowed the design to be sophisticated in fluid dynamic terms. The standard text on foil performance by Abbott and von Doenhoff (see Bibliography) showed a lift/drag ratio for the NACA 4412 section to be better than 100:1 over a wide range of conditions. Although numerous prac-

tical considerations reduce this ratio (see lift and drag analyses in Appendix) it is a good starting point. Of greater significance was the *accuracy* of the profile shape provided by an aluminium extrusion. High lift/drag performance is only generated by close conformity to the exact NACA shape, and hand-wrought foils would be difficult to make with sufficient precision whatever material was used.

The planform of the hydrofoils was comparable with that of a man-powered aircraft, using the larger of the two extrusions as the main wing and the smaller element for controlling stability. The chosen configuration, as with the Gossamer aircraft, was a canard in which the controlling element is placed well in front of the main foil, to 'feel' the water surface and set the flying height of the whole craft.

Problems unique to the sculling boat, that is not shared by propeller driven craft in air or water, are those caused by the to-and-fro movement of the sculler's centre of gravity and by the intermittent nature of the driving force. The sculling boat's extreme

Lift: drag ratio better than 100:1 as shown by the area between the straight line and the performance curve.

Canard configuration similar to Gossamer Albatross. (Photo author)

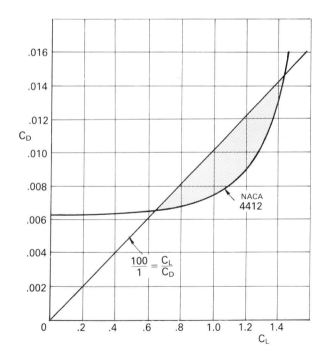

length provides an answer to the first problem, the long 'wheelbase' for the foils coping with the shift of the sculler's weight. Reassurance on the second problem was found by calculations on momentum and drag force. These indicated that the foilborne sculling craft would glide between one stroke and the next, with slight deceleration and loss of height but without the hull touching the water surface. I believed that these 'disadvantages' would be offset by the efficient use of the body's musculature while sculling, and by the efficient transfer of power from the sculler's blades which are 'locked' in the water and suffer only a small energy loss by slip, as does a propeller. There was in reality no choice, since the alternative of a cycling mechanism transferring power to a water propeller was far beyond the available time and skills. Recent information from the International Human Powered Vehicle Assn. casts doubt on both the efficiency of the sculler's movements and the energy loss of a sculling blade in water. It is likely that the cycling human power source is using his available energy more efficiently than a sculler, and a water propeller may be more efficient than an oar blade.

First trials on the water took place one early morning in May 1975. The foils had been bolted on the evening before in the seclusion of the garden, and the boat sat comfortably on an old road trailer and was easily trundled up the lane to Marlow Rowing Club. There was no-one to witness the event: total failure, should it be the result, would remain undetected. Launching singlehanded was easy, in contrast to *Icarus*' first launch, and I lifted the boat, with foils, off the trailer and into the water. After a few minutes of taxiing trials, in which the boat was predictably sluggish, all was ready for an attempt at takeoff. The thrill of anticipation was very similar to that experienced with *Icarus* six years before, but there was one major difference: this time the 'pilot' had to *provide* the power source, not merely control it. It is impossible to study the foils' performance while sculling vigorously, but despite this the first outing was a success. Full power produced takeoff and we flew for some yards, but with an impression of instability of the front foil. This instability was confirmed on a later date by Philip Hansford who observed the front foil clearing the water one moment and carrying a sheath of air deep into it the next. This ventilation proved to be a major problem, and the front foil was refashioned as a Vee with fences, very similar to those used in sailing. With this modification sustained and steady flight for ten strokes was maintained, but the energy required was that of a sprint, ruling out longer distances.

I was now prepared to venture out later in the day, when the rowing club was active, and test my speed by sculling alongside a conventional sculling boat. However, I had steering problems, finding that a tiny defect of alignment of the front foil once foilborne resulted in the boat describing a gentle arc, not correctable during the brief contact of blades with water. I had no evidence of travelling faster than a conventional sculling boat, and my Diamond Sculls fantasy began to fade slightly. Some interest had been aroused in Marlow Rowing Club and one or two expert scullers tried their hand with the foils. They did not like the experience and no-one else became foilborne: such is the power of extreme motivation. I had several more good outings, concentrating on photography and improving my technique, but my interest was beginning to wane. It seemed that much more time and effort would be needed to refine the

Sculling hydrofoil in flight, May 1975. (Photo Catherine Grogono)

foils for longer flights. I had doubts about my own further involvement and other interests supervened, the further refinement never taking place. Two years later I wrote an account for the magazines *Rowing* and *Yachts and Yachting*. An astute friend commented that I must have lost interest in winning at Henley since I made every detail available for others to copy. These publications brought a surge of interest in the mailbag. There had been several similar projects, although none had achieved successful flight.

Hard data was needed to help others pursue the project further. This required experimental evaluation of the hydrofoils, in towing tanks or moving water channels. I established contact with Southampton, Glasgow and Liverpool Universities, each of which had appropriate facilities. Dr Adrian Millward at Liverpool showed interest, and by good fortune I found that the city was also on my itinerary for a surgical conference. The spare day from the conference was spent in Dr Millward's department, and we established a link which has persisted ever since. He has supervised various student research projects which have studied the properties of the foils, albeit without pushing back the frontiers in terms of man-powered flight (see Bibliography). I was also stimulated to carry out a formal drag analysis (see Appendix), with help and advice from Leif Smitt and Dr Graham Benyon Tinker, and to present a paper at the International Symposium on High Speed Surface Craft in 1980.

The main interest in the sculling hydrofoil came and went between 1975 and 1979. Occasional correspondence continued, and there was an increasing pile of dissertations and theses from students using the foils in one or other of the test facilities. The most significant of these, apart from Liverpool, was produced by David Owers of Cambridge University and Cranfield College. He visited to discuss his project and borrowed the sculling hydrofoils, using them for a pedal and propeller configuration in which he sat semi-prone in a light kayak hull, and he just managed to fly.

In 1984 enthusiasm was rekindled. It originated in three different areas: the Royal Institute of Naval Architects (RINA), the International Human Powered Vehicle Association (IHPVA), and the Californian team of Dr Alan Abbott and Alex Brooks. The small craft division of RINA had started running annual symposia on sailing topics three years before. The subject for the fourth year was Human Powered

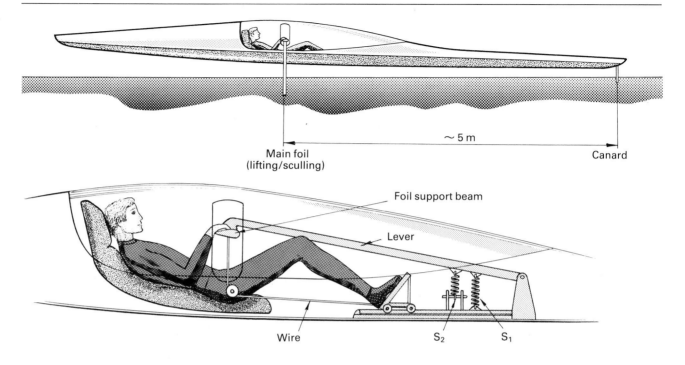

Water Vehicles, and the meeting attracted a full house for the day-long proceedings. The sculling hydrofoil was presented, as was David Owers' craft, and there was a splendid account of a Bronze Age rowing galley by Colin Mudie.

However, the craft which stole the show was that of Leif Smitt, a Danish naval architect already mentioned in Chapter 5. Leif had opted for a no-compromise design, and his sketches show the outcome. His 'hopping hydrofoil' uses the foils themselves to produce the forward force, and the human engine drives them up and down by means of to-and-fro movement of his legs, aided by strong springs to store energy at required moments in the cycle. The foil angles vary automatically to produce both lift and forward force in a manner similar to birds' wings. In fact this craft would not hop; it skimmed in an undulating manner just above the water surface, requiring only two-thirds the amount of power to match a conventional sculler at sprint speed. Its top speed would thus be considerably faster. The 'hopping hydrofoil' has not been built and may sound far-fetched. However, its designer has a good track record in the sailing hydrofoil field and his detailed design and analysis repays careful study (see Bibliography).

There has been a paucity of speed competitions for human powered water vehicles. For years such land vehicles have been refined, and competitions held, especially over a 200 m course with a flying start. Amid much activity both sides of the Atlantic, the US team seemed to win an edge, finally collecting a coveted Californian speeding ticket for travelling more than 50 miles per hour on the highway. In England the various land competitions led, in 1984, to the introduction of a water event at the Thamesmead Festival of Human Power. The initial entry form forbade craft more than 6 ft total width, specifically to exclude sculling boats. I expressed my incredulity to the organiser on the phone and the rules were relaxed to allow an entry, 'but do not collect a prize'. My sculling hydrofoil had for long been relegated to experimental use, and I had purchased a new sculling boat, a beautiful 'piece of furniture' made in cedar. It would be desecrated by attempting to attach foils. Nonetheless we took them along and placed them in a likely position under the boat, which was supported at an appropriate height. Considerable interest was aroused, right up to the moment when we lifted it into the water, without foils, and proceeded off to the course. The 'unconverted' sculling boat was considerably faster than all other entrants, and maybe the organisers were right to try and exclude such an orthodox entry.

Dr Alan Abbott on the original version of Flying Fish, *with no static flotation. (Photo Martyn Cowley)*

Steve Brooks displaying Flying Fish's *rear foil, its dimensions very similar to those of my sculling hydrofoil. (Photo Martyn Cowley)*

Dr Alan Abbott and incidence controlled front foil. (Photo Martyn Cowley)

Flying Fish *with static flotation units at Expo 86 in Vancouver. (Photo Theodore Schmidt)*

The next month saw publication in the *New Scientist* of a brief account of *Flying Fish*. This Californian project is a bicycle-like propeller driven hydrofoil, without static flotation, capable of travelling 2000 m faster than any sculler. It required a 'human catapult' and special ramp to launch, sinking on completion of the course. I soon heard that one of the team was a medical man, Dr Alan Abbott, and his collaborator Steve Brooks was an aerodynamacist from the famous man-powered flight team of *Gossamer Condor*. They were taking no chances, and the human engine was Steve Hegg, Los Angeles Olympic gold medal winner in the 4000 m cycling pursuit event.

The hydrofoil planform of *Flying Fish* was similar to the sculling hydrofoil, but the wheelbase much shorter, since there is no to-and-fro movement of the centre of gravity. Their foil dimensions were very similar to mine. They initially also used surface piercing V foils at the forward end, but opted for the greater efficiency of a surface sensing, flap-controlled, fully-submerged foil. This Californian team paid us a visit in early 1985, and returned for the much publicised 'Zapple' Festival of Human Power at Milton Keynes in late summer. Unluckily there were troubles with weed and strong wind on the only day allocated to water events, and there was no question of setting a formal record speed. The event itself was intensely reminiscent of early days of speed sailing, with a wide range of odd-looking craft varying in size, shape and number of riders. In 1986 the International Human Powered Vehicle Association held its conference and competition at Expo 86 in Vancouver. Alan Abbott rode *Flying Fish* to complete a 2000 m course in 6 minutes 40 seconds, 11 seconds faster than has ever been achieved by a sculler. He started from rest, with inflatable supports providing buoyancy, and he did not have the strong following wind which helped the sculler along on the day he had set the previous best time. Nor is he a trained athlete. Doubts about the application of hydrofoils for human power are thus resolved, but *Flying Fish* would certainly not be accepted as a Diamond Sculls entrant at Henley Royal Regatta.

CHAPTER 7

Icarus II

•

. . . with melting wax and loosened strings
Sunk hapless Icarus on unfaithful wings.
Darwin

Icarus II was designed as a hydrofoil craft to bridge the gap in size between *Icarus* and *Crossbow*. In early 1977 *Crossbow II* held the world record at 31 knots, *Icarus* and *Mayfly* held their respective class records at just over 20 knots, and the other class records were all slower. Tim Colman's resources seemed to have turned the tables on the idea that foils generate speed. How to find the extra 12 knots using our experience with *Icarus*, and the very limited resources, was the question. We believed that *Crossbow* would go even faster with foils, but Colman could not be persuaded to take the risk.

In theoretical terms hydrofoil craft do not have to be large to go fast, but an increase in size confers certain practical advantages. First is dealing with waves. A large craft, with correspondingly deep foils, would be less likely to suffer splashdowns in the waves in Portland Harbour (in 1976 the inshore course under Chesil Bank was not in regular use). Second is speed of response: a large craft cannot capsize in a trice, through a gust or coming down off her foils, and we envisaged flying in a stable manner by control of sails and steering. Large catamarans are easier to save from capsize if the windward hull lifts,

since it takes several seconds for the hull to accelerate upwards to the position of no return. Third is the lure of the open sea: I wished to explore the possibility of hydrofoil conversion of offshore multihulls and a step up in size from *Icarus* would be the best way to start this.

The first set of design sketches for *Icarus II* show an asymmetrical two-masted catamaran, resembling a scaled-down hydrofoil version of *Crossbow II*. Such a craft is dubbed 'hard-tack soft-tack' since she only sails at high speeds on one tack, returning slowly on the other one for her next run. In this respect *Crossbow II* was an improvement on the original *Crossbow*, which had only the flimsiest of rigging on the leeward side of her mast. Before making a run she had to be moored on a bridle at an angle to the wind while the sails were hoisted. Afterwards the sails were lowered while still on the same tack, for fear of being caught aback and losing the mast. A support boat then undertook the slow process of towing back to prepare for another run. However, *Icarus'* experience had shown that practicality pays, and that a speedy return for the next run plays a major part in successful campaigning at a speed event in addition to giving

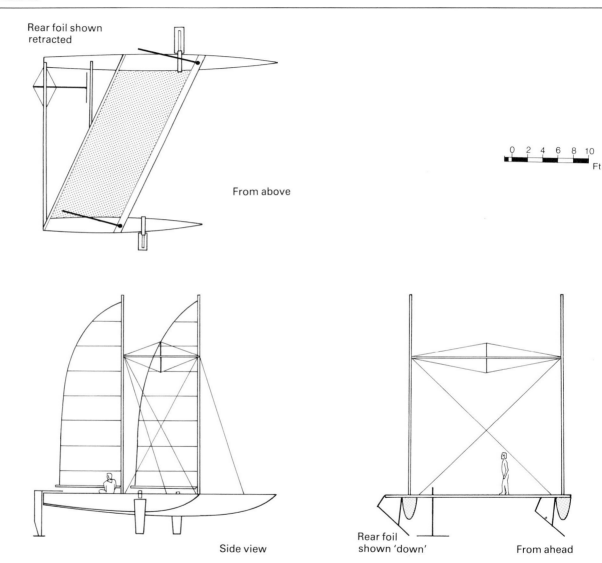

Original design sketches of Icarus II *showing an asymmetrical catamaran with rig similar to* Crossbow II *(not built).*

Rear foil shown retracted

From above

0 2 4 6 8 10
Ft

Side view

Rear foil shown 'down'

From ahead

*Final design
sketches of* Icarus
II.

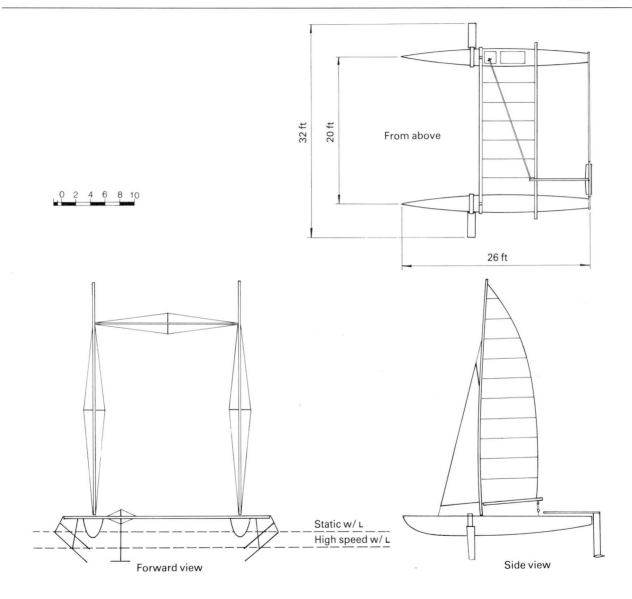

0 2 4 6 8 10

32 ft

20 ft

From above

26 ft

Static w/ L

High speed w/ L

Forward view

Side view

more enjoyment and placing less reliance on support craft. For this reason the final designs of *Icarus II* show a symmetrical 26 ft long catamaran, 20 ft in beam without foils and 32 ft with them. A small degree of asymmetry is seen in the position of the rear foil close to one hull, the leeward hull on a speed run. This feature was intended to improve stability at high speed, and full symmetry could be produced quite easily by moving the foil to a central position if desired.

The design was simplified by using ready-made components where possible. The rig consists of two Tornado sailplans set side by side 18 ft apart. For the purpose of calculating loss of performance because of proximity of the sails, the rig may be regarded as a biplane. The calculated loss was found to be less than 5% since the sailplans are more than two chord lengths in their average separation. The hulls are scaled-up Tornado hulls. The increase in overall length from 20 to 26 ft, with corresponding increases in beam and depth, doubles the enclosed volume of each hull. This provides an ample reserve of displacement while not foilborne. The materials used were of similar grade to the Tornado, thus increasing the weight of each hull by only 70% or slightly less since centreboard boxes were unnecessary. The cross-beams were scaled up only a little in relation to the Tornado, despite the craft's overall beam being doubled. This saving in weight and windage was made possible by the rig being split between the two hulls; the extreme bending load on the centre of a normal Tornado's front crossbeam is absent.

The hydrofoils were designed on similar lines to *Icarus'*, with a planned takeoff speed of 15 knots. The calculated top speed was over 30 knots, since each feature contributing to speed had been significantly improved in comparison with *Icarus*. With twice the power, less than twice the weight, and more than four times the stability, *Icarus II* was designed to use the proven advantages of hydrofoils for the purpose of taking the World Sailing Speed Record.

With the design complete there was 'merely' the problem of finance and building. Although a search for a main sponsor was unsuccessful, the reputation of *Icarus* could be used for low level sponsorship in the supply of masts, sails and rigging. A group of friends were willing to form a new syndicate similar to the *Icarus* team, the principle being that a small cash contribution from each member earns the right to put in much unpaid hard work, and in return share the fun of campaigning in speed events and possibly winning prize money. The project seemed very speculative and I was only willing to accept £100 from each member, allowing for the possibility of a total loss in the first year. The suppliers of free materials would also be made equal 'owners' in recognition of their contributions, but a cash fund of £600 left us a long way short of buying hulls and foils, which we could not make for ourselves.

During the first few weeks of 1977 we had a stroke of luck. Ben Wynne, now owner of *Mayfly*, was a postgraduate student at Newcastle University in the Department of Naval Architecture. Ben had established contact with the training and safety company of Swan Hunter Shipbuilders, in particular the managing director Colin Douglas with whom he was collaborating in the modification of *Mayfly* with a view to making a commercial version. A message was sent through Ben indicating the nature of our problem with *Icarus II*. Colin then telephoned and offered help. He had been a Master Mariner in earlier years, but left the sea when a young family arrived, and

joined Swan Hunters. His unit consisted of 200 apprentices and 20 instructors who taught basic wood and metalworking skills as applied to shipbuilding. Colin's proposition was this: his apprentices were working in wood and metal under the guidance of expert instructors. If we paid for the materials they would produce the hulls and foils for *Icarus II* without labour costs. In round terms this required £1000, and Colin and his friend Brian Sample offered to sponsor us for half. We thus had to produce £500, a sum already in hand, and the building of *Icarus II* could go ahead. The syndicate of owners had 14 members, each contributing either £100 or some major component (see Appendix).

In April 1977 I sent Colin the designs and building instructions for *Icarus II*. These consisted of 20 sheets of scruffy hand-written paper, such was my lack of time and expertise. I made one visit to Colin's firm during construction; a large area had been taken over for the construction of *Icarus II* and his team seemed enthused. I blushed more than once as a senior instructor opened a drawer and took out well-thumbed photocopies of my 20 sheets of scribble. He would politely ask me to interpret some particularly obscure part of it, which I would then try to do, and we would move on. It was a summer of industrial unrest generally, and even the training company became involved: the boat was the object of mild industrial action which caused long delays. However, Colin's enthusiasm and diplomacy ensured that the bare hulls and foils were completed and delivered in August, much later than the original schedule but still six weeks before Speed Week.

Each 26 ft hull could readily be lifted by a man at either end; they weighed 100 kg each, and the other components weighed in as expected to produce a total displacement very near 500 kg or just less than half a ton (see Appendix). No craft of overall dimensions 26 × 32 ft had ever been built down to anything like this weight, but it remained to be seen whether or not the structure would withstand actual sailing forces in strong winds. Because of time constraints the front foils had been subject to major modification. Colin had developed an aluminium extrusion with 8 in chord for the commercial version of *Mayfly*, and had been obliged to use this ready-made material as a quicker and cheaper alternative to fabrication. Thus the front foils had become a two-rung ladder, causing us some concern that they might have lost strength, but we had no alternative.

Scale diagram of Icarus II's main foil geometry with hacksaw tuning points.

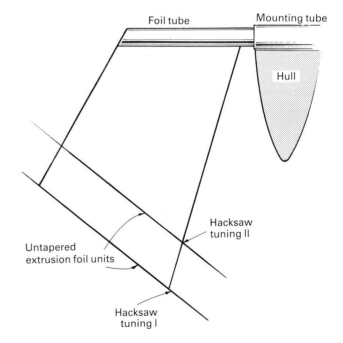

During our wait for the hulls and foils the Marlow-based members of the team structured the rig. The two Tornado masts required major modification to stand side by side 18 ft apart. Derek Lessware, a locally based aeronautical engineer, made a huge contribution to the rig and rigging. He supplied the standing rigging as sponsorship by his firm Sarma UK, and he made a model which demonstrated the effect of the rig on the platform of hulls and cross-beams: the addition of the rig transformed this floppy structure into a rigid framework. Also he designed the complex fitting which would accommodate the high-level crossbeam and yet allow the masts to over-rotate. Over-rotation, in which the spar is turned into the wind and farther, affecting the sail shape, is vital, since it gives the lee side of a Tornado rig its wing-like curvature. Derek and I often agreed, and often disagreed. He felt his engineering expertise must hold sway; I often thought he was using excessive safety standards that were more appropriate to aircraft. This I believed unnecessary since numerous strength failures had occurred with *Icarus* and had never injured life or limb.

The last six weeks of sustained effort transformed the bare hulls into a boat ready to sail. The first half of this time was spent in a large engineering depot where space and much other help was provided by the firm's proprietor, John Mitchell. We had a level floor indoors with excellent light. Placing and fitting attachment chocks for the crossbeams was thus made easy, as was painting the hulls. We then moved to our front garden, which was completely filled by the boat. Fitting the rig, rigging, winches, sheeting points, trampoline and all other equipment took far longer than anticipated. I felt obliged to complete the boat for that year's Speed Week, and we started work-

ing 16 hour days. A shift system allowed each of the team to do eight hours of his regular employment a day, and spend eight hours on *Icarus II*. A buildup of stress and fatigue occurred, obscured by enthusiasm and the need to meet the deadline. Derek Lessware, John Anderson and Ted Casson seemed to work at all hours, one or more of them often there as I retired, after midnight, or before I was up in the morning. Ted in particular bore with patience the brunt of my irritability, which was often directed at him for the simple reason that he was always there to help. Relationships within the family suffered, but a reasonable state of readiness was achieved. We set off with two well-laden cars and trailers, and one spare day to re-assemble *Icarus II* at Portland Harbour.

That year, 1977, was a vintage one for speed sailing. *Crossbow II* had her first full week of campaigning after having been barely completed the year

before, and she broke her own world record with a speed of 33·8 knots. On the same day a new era was introduced by a sailboard raising the 10 sq metre Class record to 19·6 knots, an increase of 4 knots over the existing record. The young Dutchman Derk Thijs achieved this on a standard production hull over lumpy water inside Portland Harbour. Confident assertions were made that this 'freak' speed would be difficult to repeat and that it represented extreme athletic skill in one individual. On the same day *Icarus* put the B Class world record up to 22·2 knots in the hands of Andrew Grogono. The inshore course was also open for the first time and enabled *Mayfly* to raise the A Class record to 23 knots.

Icarus II had a mixed week, with numerous breakages, but some exciting moments of high speed. On the first day we attempted to sail in a gusty Force 5 northerly, and folded the port front foil under the boat. The design had allowed the foil to be tucked in under the hull too much, and the changes required to accommodate the extrusion had further weakened it. Repair seemed out of the question, but the team soon had the modifications made to attempt high speed on the other tack, ignoring the bent foil. An exact repetition occurred, with the foil bending in under the hull, and it was difficult to see how the damage could possibly be repaired and the necessary extra strength provided. However, I underestimated the enthusiasm of Derek Lessware, who mobilised local engineering resources in the form of Granby Precision. The foils reappeared after one day's absence, a great deal stronger than they had ever been, and there were no more fold-ups. *Icarus II* became foilborne with ease in wind of Force 4 and above, but there were two stability problems. The first concerned flying too high, and we executed several dramatic slewing turns to windward when the rudder foil came so high out of the water that its last remaining fence was no longer immersed. This problem was solved by 'hacksaw tuning' the front foils, sawing off first one and then the other unsupported lower ends as a means of reducing flying height. The second problem was caused by a tendency to go nose-down. This was more difficult to diagnose but quite serious in preventing sustained flight. Because of her size this instability developed slowly, and could be corrected if the tailplane was under manual control as in an aircraft. Again I thought this was beyond our resources, but Derek Lessware proved me wrong, producing in one day's work a 'fully flying' tailplane, one which moved as a whole to alter the angle of incidence rather than using control flaps as in aircraft. The wind departed before we had fully evaluated this change. The week's sailing left us all with a feeling of great potential for *Icarus II*, but she was very labour intensive both ashore and in the water when compared with similar smaller craft such as *Icarus* and *Mayfly*. In particular raising the masts with their high level crossbeam seemed to require six strong men and good co-ordination.

With Speed Week over it became clear that I had run into borrowed time in terms of physical and mental reserves. A variety of stress symptoms, and a feeling that the family seemed distant, led me to resolve not to let the same thing happen again: hobby interests thenceforth must stay secondary to work and family. A year passed, with *Icarus II* safely stored, and enthusiasm for further sailing was rekindled by the Marlow team which included Derek Lessware, John Anderson, Ted Casson and myself. Modifications included the installation of a horizontal

Icarus II *at speed in stable flight (1977). (Photo Guy Gurney)*

joystick; this looked like a normal boat's tiller and sideways movements produced the usual effect. However, in the vertical axis it controlled the fully flying tailplane and thus the flying height. This invention worked well but was somewhat heavy in the hand. We went to Weymouth for a short week of trial sailing in June 1979 but were dogged by light winds. Speed Week that year also lacked wind and our improvements were not fully evaluated. I then resigned from the syndicate: *Icarus II* was one commitment too many. Derek Lessware's enthusiasm was unquenchable and he took over. The original boat's shareholders were offered their money back but none accepted, all insisting they had had good value for their contribution. Derek embarked on further modifications, which included new foils and new control mechanisms. There was uncertainty about the financing of this operation, and in due course the original syndicate asked to be retired, thus being relieved of further financial involvement. Derek involved a friend of his, Bob Downhill, and together with several others they set out to improve and campaign *Icarus II*. The following is a summary of their account.

New main foils were structured out of mild steel to a computer-assisted design by Bob Downhill. The foils' angle of attack was adjusted by means of a lever arm and screw thread, and several outings on Queen Mary's Reservoir proved that they worked well. Speed Week in 1980 came at a bad time for Derek Lessware. After two good but untimed runs on the first day, a series of disasters culminated in a glorious cartwheel in Portland Harbour. *Icarus II* finally sank to the seabed. One of several reasons for the disaster was a lack of the right helmsman (myself, J. G.) when most needed. The boat had been wrecked and repaired twice already that week, but the third mishap was a divers' job. Thanks to H.M. Navy and Bucks Diving School she was brought ashore, and due to a depressed financial situation she spent the next three years on land and in total disrepair.

Bob Downhill came to *Icarus II*'s rescue in 1983, rebuilding her with a Southall based team. His policy had been to accrue sea time and no design improvements were attempted. In 1984 he took her to Brest Speed Week. By now the boat had become a much repaired version of her former pristine self. Nevertheless she has performed well, and her crew have had many foilborne hours with her. Bob has continued to sail her from Calshot in the summers, and at Weymouth Speed Week each autumn. In the summer of 1986 she foundered again while sailing off Calshot and

Icarus II, refitted in June 1979, makes a good platform for a party of ten in the absence of strong wind.

Icarus II *in 1980, foilborne in the hands of Derek Lessware and Bob Downhill.*

repair seemed unlikely. However, Bob effected a further repair, and Speed Week saw the reappearance of a now tired looking craft.

Icarus II has shown how great are the demands made in maintaining and campaigning a large and unwieldy craft. The large size of the syndicate, and their tiny financial input at my request, had heightened these difficulties. Despite her failure to ever make a run at high speed across the course, few doubt that her overall concept is a likely one, and a well financed version might prove very successful.

CHAPTER 8

Icarus over the Years

•

Icarus, my son, I charge you to keep at a moderate height, for if you fly too low the damp will clog your wings, and if too high the heat will melt them.

Daedalus

Far and away the longest survivor of successive Weymouth Speed Weeks is *Icarus*. In the first 15 years of this annual event she entered 13 times and won her Class prize on each occasion. For the first 10 years she was also near the front in overall results, never finishing below third except in 1979 when one Tornado hull 'exploded' early in the week and repair was out of the question. In early years the first three positions were often shared with one of the *Crossbow*s and with *Mayfly*, but from 1982 onwards the sailboards have dominated. *Icarus* came closest to outright victory in Speed Week in 1980 and 1981, on each occasion being within one fifth of a knot of the sailboard which made the fastest run of the week.

On the negative side, *Icarus*' increases in speed have been modest compared with those in other classes; her initial speed of 21·6 knots in 1972 has been increased to 28·2 knots over 15 years, while the speed of one or other *Crossbow* increased from 26·3 to 36 knots and the sailboards from 15 knots to 38·9 knots. The explanation for this modest rise lies mainly in equipment, *Icarus* changing relatively little while both larger and smaller classes have introduced fundamental new designs.

B Class World Sailing Speed Record Holders

1974	*Orlando*	16·3 knots
1975	Hobie 16	16·9 knots
1976	*Icarus*	20·7 knots
1977	*Icarus*	22·2 knots
1978	nf^2	23·0 knots
1980	*Icarus*	23·8 knots
1981	*Icarus*	24·5 knots
1983	*Icarus*	26·6 knots
1983	*Icarus*	28·1 knots

Unlimited Class World Sailing Speed Record Holders

1972	*Crossbow*	26·3 knots
1973	*Crossbow*	29·3 knots
1975	*Crossbow*	31·1 knots
1976	*Crossbow II*	31·8 knots
1977	*Crossbow II*	33·8 knots
1980	*Crossbow II*	36·0 knots
1986	Pascal Maka on sailboard	38·9 knots

What have been the main changes which evolved in *Icarus* over the years? There are three main areas, concerning the Tornado itself, the front foils and the rear foils. The Tornado catamaran has undergone remarkable improvements since 1967. In early years attention was given mainly to improving structural details, following the breakages and failures which were inevitable in subjecting such a light and powerful craft to tough racing conditions. It became both popular and durable, which led to selection for the Olympics in 1976 and every subsequent Olympiad. The stimulus of top level competition produced major improvements in the rig, which has become far more efficient despite the limitation of one-design rules. Thus the winning Tornado of each Olympics has become out-dated during the subsequent four years by advances in rig design. *Icarus* has benefited by using each innovation as it came along. We have been fortunate in acquiring cast-offs from top competitors, often around the time when one Olympic campaign has just been completed.

Icarus has required new hulls on two occasions, a new mast on six, and new sails five times during 15 years. In addition the trampoline has been replaced

Icarus *passing the central marker of the Portland Course in 1980, when the 'wheelbase' of her foils was only 10 ft.*

three times, the rudders twice, and the rear beam
once, leaving only the front beam and centreboards
as components of the original Tornado. Alongside
this quick turnover of Tornado parts the foils seem
quite durable, the original metal front foils of 1972
surviving to the present time, and the rear ones being
modified or rebuilt on two occasions. However, their
position has altered greatly, and the Appendix shows
the changes of front and rear foils over the years.
Both sets of foils have moved aft, each move giving
an increase in stability as the loading on them has
become more like that of an aeroplane with the main
load carried on the front wings and the rear ones providing control. This shift of the foils has corrected
an original misconception about the danger of
forward somersaulting. We initially thought that the
driving force from the rig would make such pitch-
poling likely, but the risk was exaggerated and it
seems *less* likely with all the foils moved aft. The
change in position of the rear foils was also necessary
to restore the length of wheelbase. The photo shows
an anxious Alan Grogono passing the central buoy
of the open water course at speed while trying to control *Icarus* in the 'close coupled' version of 1980.
Thereafter the rear foil moved back on an extension
frame 2 ft behind the hulls, and then a further 2 ft
with a marked gain in stability.

Icarus' second year of speed sailing was a disap-
pointment; so-called improvements consisted of
extending the front foil mountings outwards to provide more beam, converting the double rear foil
system to a single central one, copying Philip
Hansford's *Mayfly*, and an extra-large low-set foresail. Despite these changes our top speed at Portland
went down from 21·6 to 20 knots while *Crossbow*'s
went up from 26 to 29 knots. We also suffered major

Icarus *on a timed run during 1973 Speed Week, showing oversized foresail and unusual crewing positions. (Photo* Yachting World)

FAR RIGHT *Nigel Irens sailing* Clifton Flasher: *excellent aerofoils but no hydrofoils. (Photo* Yachting World)

stability problems, even in calm water, made worse in strong winds by the waves invariably found in the middle of Portland Harbour. Hydrofoils proved popular with other competitors, 13 of the 17 entrants having some form of foils on their craft. Although *Icarus'* performance was disappointing she was second fastest of the week, more than 2 knots faster than the C class catamaran, *Lady B*, which came third. We decided to start a campaign for the introduction of class prizes for the smaller craft, and for an inshore course to be set up under Chesil Bank, resolving to await such changes before re-entering the competition.

In the following two years *Icarus* was absent from Speed Week. The 1974 event saw no new records, and interest centred on the battle for top speed between the big catamaran *British Oxygen* (24·3 knots) and the revolutionary *Clifton Flasher* (22·1 knots). The latter could only sail on starboard tack and set a rigid five-part wingsail. *Mayfly* (19·4 knots) was the only other craft exceeding 17 knots despite an abundance of strong winds. In 1975 prizes of £125 were introduced for small sail area classes, and 21 entrants achieved 344 timed runs – itself a record. *Crossbow* exceeded 30 knots on several occasions, setting a new world record of 31·1 knots. Once again the only other craft faster than 17 knots was *Mayfly* (19·4 knots). The B Class was won by a Hobie 16 at just under 17 knots. The absence of *Icarus* was lamented by Bob Fisher in a *Yachts & Yachting* report.

The Weymouth competition now suffered because of a lack of competition for *Crossbow*, and the initial failure of the class prizes to attract entries capable of a reasonably fast speed. However, weather continued to favour the event, and the first four years of good winds were followed by two more. Both 1976 and 1977 saw an increased number of entrants and timed runs. In each of these years *Crossbow II* set a new Open Class record (31·8 and 33·8 knots); *Mayfly* recorded the second fastest speed, setting A Class records (21·1 and 23·0 knots); and *Icarus* recorded the third fastest time, setting new B Class records (20·7 and 22·2 knots). In 1977 the B Class competition had a good year; I was busy with *Icarus II*, leaving Andrew Grogono shorthanded. Alan Grog was there to help him set a new record, but on some days he lacked a crew; a photo shows him singlehanded, leaping out of the water in a gust while *Icarus II* steams past apparently in excellent control.

Despite a high level of satisfaction from competitors, and a well-established position in the sailing calendar, Speed Week was in jeopardy. John Players had become disenchanted with the lack of return in terms of publicity, and the event did not fit easily into their scheme of sponsorship; speed sailing was too small to be considered for 'special event' status and thus its administration was run directly by the company's own public relations department. From the RYA side there was a hardening policy against cigarettes, and Players ceased sponsorship in 1977. As an added complication Tim Colman was now hesitant about continuing his campaign with *Crossbow II*: it made little sense to continue putting in so much time and effort without significant competition.

Two windless years followed: 1978 and 1979 both had ample numbers of entrants, the list being closed at 50 to reduce long delays while awaiting a run. Only one entrant at a time could use the course and a booking system was necessary, each craft often waiting more than an hour between one attempt and the next. In early years there were few craft capable of staying

at sea for long, but sailboards soon showed their ability to survive in all conditions. Boardsailors were quite willing to make a series of runs only five minutes apart. Thus frustration built up, and it was clear that some form of electronic timing was necessary. It was already in use for time-trial events in the rowing world, where 500 rowing eights could start at 10 second intervals and be timed and allocated placings without difficulty, and a strong case was made for transferring to a similar system.

Icarus competed throughout the windless years, mixing the frustrations of slow timing and only moderate winds with much enjoyment at simply being foilborne; a typical run across the timed course would be followed by being unable to stop, and continuing the whole width of Portland Harbour before reluctantly coming off the foils. On one occasion we went to sea, continuing a speed run through the entrance of Portland Harbour and 6 miles along the coast to Lulworth Cove. This sea passage was made with Colin Douglas. *Icarus*' sea-keeping abilities were impressive: the wind was southerly between 12 and 15 knots, with 3 ft waves. The foils produced a cushioned ride; they failed to keep the hulls fully clear of the water, but gave a far faster and dryer ride than we would have had without them. Although the hulls touched the wave tops their slender shape prevented too much drag, and we felt safe on the foils in the open sea. From that time on I became convinced that hydrofoils could be used on modern offshore multihulls, especially since these big multis shared with the Tornado the features which originally made it seem so suitable: a wide platform with a huge sailplan and very light displacement. In 1978 *Icarus* (19·5 knots) once again came second to *Crossbow* (27·7 knots). The event had started without a

Abandoned by the author in favour of Icarus II (foreground), Andrew Grogono has control problems sailing Icarus singlehanded (background).

Crossbow II *won
every Speed Week
she entered,
regardless of wind
strength.*

sponsor, and although Smirnoff came in at the last moment their interest lasted only one year.

Tim Colman then withdrew, and 1979 was the low point in the history of the event: no sponsor, no strong wind and no *Crossbow*. Again I had abandoned *Icarus* to concentrate on *Icarus II*, and Andrew Grog enlisted heavyweight round-the-world sailor Ian Worley, confident that his power and weight on the trapeze would make a new record if strong winds arrived. On the Wednesday *Icarus* made several runs at around 19 knots and then Ian Worley began to exert himself. He and Andrew set *Icarus* into the timed section, very tight sheeted in 15 knots of wind, and disaster struck: the rig tension tore apart the leeward hull, the front 8 ft being completely discon-

Icarus sheds the front 8 ft of her leeward hull; the separated piece is visible under the foresail. (Photo Stephen Baker)

nected. The main foil remained attached under the boat by its control wires, and a lengthy salvage job ended with all three foils present and intact. The week finished with no new records, but the course was kept open for the boardsailors whose commercial backers encouraged them to wait any length of time in the chance of setting a new record. The Dutchman Jaap van de Rest set a new record of 22·3 knots the day after Speed Week, and Englishman Clive Colenso achieved 22·9 knots the next day. There then followed a year-long argument about the accuracy of the timing of Colenso's run, and although his record was verified it was agreed that more stringent control would be needed in the future.

In 1980 the pattern of Speed Week changed. Sailboards began to dominate, both in the numerical sense and in achieving the fastest speeds. The introduction of computer-controlled timing allowed competitors to enter the course with only 20-second gaps and their frustrations were thereby eased. Committee Chairman Sir Reginald Bennett and RYA Race Manager John Reed stood beaming and beckoning competitors into the course. On the first day winds were light, allowing much needed practice with the timing system, but on the second day the wind blew for the first time in three years and a new era started. In the late afternoon *Icarus* ran repeatedly across the course at an estimated speed of around 19 knots, only to come ashore and find that we had reached 23·2 knots – only a fraction below the B Class record. It was then held by Prof. Bradfield with nf^2 and we regretted our lack of resolve in not pushing ourselves and the boat harder. We were in luck, however, with strong winds throughout the week, and Alan Grogono crewed by David Pelly set a new record at 23·8 knots. This was the only record made that week,

since boardsailor Jaap van de Rest (23·9 knots) did not equal his own record made earlier in Hawaii.

That year the event was sponsored by sailboard manufacturers Ten Cate Sports. Just over half of the competitors reached a respectable speed in excess of 16 knots, and with Ten Cate offering a second year's support the future of Speed Week was secure once more. The *Icarus* syndicate had particular interest in its continuation, since it is doubtful whether the foils would have been brought out of store each year without this stimulus. After Speed Week was over Tim Colman made a major attempt to better his own record and reached 36 knots, subsequently announcing his retirement from the sport.

The next year, 1981, was the first of several held in extremely strong winds. *Icarus* enjoyed new-found stability by moving the rear foil back 2 ft, and was again the only craft to make a new record during the week, recording 24·5 knots with Andrew Grogono helming and myself as crew. It would be nice to suggest that we contributed equally to this record, but the photo suggests the true story. I had previously been convinced that hydrofoil sailing must be physically challenging, with the helmsman fully extended on a trapeze, preferably singlehanded; tiller in one hand, mainsheet in the other and foresheet between the teeth. Instead we found that *Icarus* was often more stable with the crew inboard and the foresheet cleated, since the tension was too great to move it once speed had built up. It was also impossible to adjust the mainsheet when inboard simply because there are no footholds on the trampoline and pulling it in caused one to slide aft out of control. The record run was thus made with me lying flat on my back admiring our wake and Andrew's anxious face, but making no other contribution. It was the only time

I have been on board for a record run.

Sailboard domination had taken over with a vengeance, 28 of the 41 entries being boards. The lure of speed-boarding was difficult to resist: the result was a home-made 9 ft board called *Dots* after my younger daughter Dorothy. Both weighed in at 7 kg. *Dots* was cut and shaped from a high-density polystyrene foam block by means of a hot wire wielded by Geoff Keane. Geoff is an ex-dinghy sailor and engineering genius whose skills have con-

tributed to all the craft I have laid claim to in this book, although his greatest expertise is in heavier tasks such as rebuilding traction engines. He quickly learned to glide the hot wire through a block of polystyrene, guided by templates tacked on either side of the block. Having shaped the profile and deck plan in this way, the hard angles were rounded and the shape was complete. I covered the polystyrene in a sheath of epoxy-impregnated Kevlar and a very strong board resulted. Designing and shaping the skeg involved us in some familiar 'hydrofoil' work, but we chose not to introduce experimental features since we did not wish to risk getting it wrong. *Dots* proved easy to sail, and I reached 18·9 knots before handing over to National Champion Dee Caldwell, who recorded a speed of 23·2 knots. This was the fastest speed by an Englishman in 1981, but the German Jürgen Hönscheid (24·7 knots) and two others were just a little faster. Speed-board design evolved so rapidly that *Dots* was a long way out of date by the following year.

There was no respite for *Icarus* despite her new record, and Andrew Grog entered for the first Brest Speed Week which took place two weeks later. The French had found a much higher level of media interest and sponsorship. The entrepreneur was Charles le Moing of Dacmar, who had called on us a year before when collecting information. The French agreed to use identical rules, and have done so ever since, although this has tested the political skills of Sir Reginald Bennett on occasion. Brest lacks the natural protection of Portland Harbour, and the water is always even more lumpy in strong winds. This gave an advantage to the large ocean-going multihulls, several of which were entered, but the *Icarus* team were by now familiar with slightly awkward conditions. Andrew Grog was crewed by David Pelly in the first half of the week and Alan Chilvers in the second, and won outright with a speed of 23·4 knots. The 10 sq m Class was won by *Seafly* at 19·6 knots, and the sailboard class by Erica Keller who beat all the men with a speed of just over 20 knots. Andrew brought home prize money worth £4,500 and the syndicate had some difficulty in deciding what to do with it. Eventually it was agreed not to share it out, nor spend it all on one major development. Instead a fund was established to cover all *Icarus'* expenses and entry fees, and there has not been a further need for a kitty.

Portland Speed Week was unsponsored in 1982, although an unofficial speed event at the same venue the week before had been supported by Johnnie Walker. Despite primitive accommodation ashore and a timing system that was tested to the limit, this RYA Speed Week was a success; sailboards filled the first ten places, all at speeds over 25 knots. The world record was broken by six of them, and the winner Pascal Maka made runs of over 27 knots three times on the same afternoon. A new C Class record of 25·0 knots was also set by *Jacob's Ladder* using a stack of kites instead of a sailplan. *Icarus* had an unlucky week with mast breakages and failure of a new rear foil. It had been designed slightly longer, to keep the inverted T piece adequately immersed at very high speeds, but had not been built according to our instructions. A welded joint had been made halfway down and, not surprisingly, it failed when subjected to the full bending load. This was the only failure of metal foils that has ever occurred with *Icarus*, and the replacement, built as designed, has lasted to the present without trouble.

The representatives of Johnnie Walker stayed on to watch RYA Speed Week and in due course agreed to a generous three year sponsorship, probably renewable thereafter, which has restored stability to the event. A veritable village of Portacabins and hospitality trailers now appears in the carpark opposite Chesil Beach, and Johnnie Walker's seem pleased with the level of publicity.

In recent years *Icarus* has remained unchanged. The funds would provide for new front foils, but a design conference failed to find any way of improving significantly on their design. We therefore agreed to continue refurbishing them, and keep the money in hand to pay ever-increasing entry fees. In 1983 *Icarus* raised the B Class record to 26·6 knots, in the hands of Andrew Grog crewed by John Fowler, while sailboarder Fred Haywood reached 30·8 knots, the first time that 30 knots had been exceeded by a board. The 1984 week started with three windless days, and *Icarus* had another mast breakage when the wind arrived on the fourth day. No records were broken in a week noticeable by the absence of larger craft, but there were many sailboards to take their places.

A variety of experimental craft returned in 1985 and the event ran very smoothly thanks to Johnnie Walker's sponsorship and a sophisticated timing mechanism comparable to any found on the Continent. *Icarus* was the only craft to break a record, reaching 28·2 knots in the hands of Andrew Grog and Johnathan Fowler (son of syndicate member John Fowler). I was languishing in a hospital bed in Oxford, having had an operation to remove a slipped disc the previous week. *Icarus'* speed was probably increased by this bit of personal ill fortune, since Andrew reported that Johnathan refused to free the mainsheet when the wind increased: 'He wouldn't let the damned thing go'. Since *Icarus* is now in a fully

Analysis of Icarus'
*speed in 81 timed
runs at the 1985
Portland Speed
Week.*

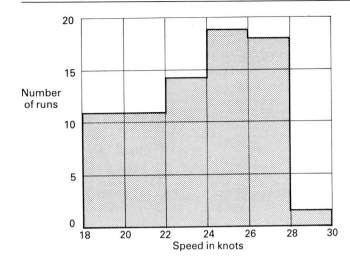

evolved state, with a reasonable margin of both strength and stability, the result of Johnathan's intransigence was an inevitable increase in speed. *Icarus* made 81 timed runs on the five best days, and the graph showing how these were distributed makes the importance of repeated runs very obvious: a sequence of up to 20 or 30 runs might have taken place without any of them being above 28 knots. The publicity department of Johnnie Walker made much of *Icarus'* record, since it was the only one, and the syndicate enjoyed the limelight on the podium of the Earls Court Boat Show where Sir Reginald Bennett presented Andrew and Johnathan with their prize.

In 1986 the *Icarus* syndicate teamed up with Gifford Technology in making an A Class wing rig. The rig was designed by Austin Farrar along similar lines to the *Lady Helmsman* C Class rig of 20 years ago, and was built by Nick Barlow. He made the wing strong enough to withstand 60 knots of apparent wind, and fate took its vengeance by producing a Speed Week in which the wind never exceeded 12 knots after the first morning. The BBC had made a persuasive case for on-board cameras, and that morning was spent making runs with two cameras mounted. We made one run of 21·9 knots, but by then the wind was lessening and the tape securing one of the cameras was causing a lot of spray. We came ashore to remove the cameras, unaware that the best conditions of the week had already finished. The *Icarus* team spent the rest of the week practising the change from Tornado rig to wing rig, and in making new friends and meeting old ones among the several hundred people who commit themselves to Speed Week each year whether there is wind or not.

Icarus' *wing rig shown here being tested by Reg White following a windless 1986 Speed Week. (Photo Clarence Farrar)*

CHAPTER 9

Daydreams and Dinosaurs

•

I had a dream, which was not all a dream.
Byron

Up to this point the projects described have been both practical and attainable. Objectives have been limited by the people and resources available, and a conservative approach has been rewarded by a fair measure of success. What more ambitious projects remain untried? The list is a long one. It starts with projects most likely to succeed, and progresses to the more extreme flights of fancy. First come the hydrofoil conversions of a C Class catamaran, both for speed sailing, and for attempts to regain the Little America's Cup. Second is conversion of *Catapult*, the production version of John Montgomery's inflatable car-top catamaran. Third is hydrofoil conversion of a modern lightweight offshore multihull like *Paragon* or *Apricot*, with the initial objective of increasing speed at sea in favourable conditions and a more ambitious objective of winning Round-the-Wight or Round Britain Races. Fourth takes us to the other end of the size scale: developing tiny foils to fly sailboards on very flat water and evaluate their speed potential. Fifth is the refinement of *Icarus*' foils, to try and outsail a standard Tornado round a triangular course, given sufficient wind to be foilborne. Sixth is the hydrofoil conversion of *Crossbow II*, and

last is the 'blank cheque project'. This is the design and development of an offshore *purpose-built* hydrofoil, not a conversion, given ample resources to use modern materials and expertise in all aspects of the project.

There is a short list of deliberate omissions. No place is given for attempts at commercial load-carrying on foils, and there is no place for foil stabilisation, as opposed to flying. There is no attempt to market hydrofoils as a bolt-on extra for an existing design, and even less an attempt to market a purpose-built sailing hydrofoil as a commercial venture. The omissions show a bias against any form of commercial application, and also against stabilisation by foils.

Top of the list of untried projects comes the hydrofoil conversion of a C Class catamaran. This requires only a small extension of the *Icarus* project, since the Tornado is in B Class and C Class is the next one up in size. However, there have been profound differences in their development. B Class has been dominated by the Tornado one-design, and no major changes have ever been allowed in the shape of the hulls or the general arrangements of the boat or its rig. By contrast there has never been a one-design in C Class, and the only active racing during the same 20 years has been for the Little America's Cup (LAC), an international challenge trophy modelled on the lines of the much better known 12 Metre America's Cup. Won by Great Britain from the USA in the first contest in 1961, the LAC was defended successfully against seven challenges but left these shores for Denmark in 1969. The following year it was won by Australia; I was sent to Copenhagen by *Yachting World* to cover the event. In the mid-1970s the LAC went to the USA, and stayed there until Australia regained it in 1985, and retained it in 1987.

The development of C Class cats in the early 1980s has been dramatic: the use of modern materials has halved displacement from around 1200 to around 600 lb, and the power and efficiency of the rigid wing rigs have been much improved. Each advance in performance makes it more likely that hydrofoils will be effective, since foils only come into their own when the drag of displacement hulls starts to rise steeply at around 15 knots. In early 1986 I published the design of a C Class hydrofoil. The hulls are smaller, shorter and lighter than usual, since they do not carry major loads or stresses once foilborne. The rig consists of a 'biplane' of two parallel masts with their tips canted towards each other. Such a biplane incurs no disadvantage once the two components are two chord lengths apart, and the centre of effort is brought down with benefit to stability while foilborne. Each component of this rig is designed as a scaled-down version of the state of art rigid C Class rigs, benefiting from the advances made in Australia and the USA.

The hydrofoils are small (total area 7 sq ft) since there is no advantage in becoming foilborne at speeds of less than around 14 knots, and above this the

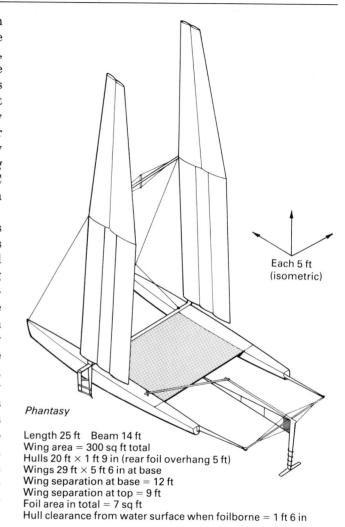

Each 5 ft
(isometric)

Phantasy

Length 25 ft   Beam 14 ft
Wing area = 300 sq ft total
Hulls 20 ft × 1 ft 9 in (rear foil overhang 5 ft)
Wings 29 ft × 5 ft 6 in at base
Wing separation at base = 12 ft
Wing separation at top = 9 ft
Foil area in total = 7 sq ft
Hull clearance from water surface when foilborne = 1 ft 6 in

Velocity triangles
showing expected
apparent wind
effect for Phantasy,
*when beam-
reaching, tacking
downwind and
upwind.* (Yachts
and Yachting)

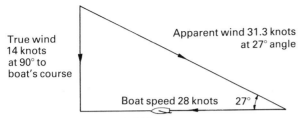

True wind
14 knots
at 90° to
boat's course

Apparent wind 31.3 knots
at 27° angle

Boat speed 28 knots   27°

Velocity triangle expected of *Phantasy*
on a beam reach in 14 knots true wind.

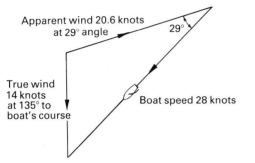

Apparent wind 20.6 knots
at 29° angle   29°

True wind
14 knots
at 135° to
boat's course

Boat speed 28 knots

Velocity triangle on a downwind 'tack' in 14 knots true wind.

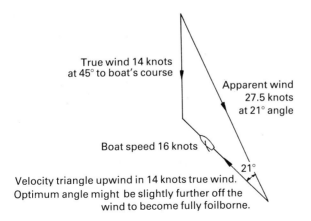

True wind 14 knots
at 45° to boat's course

Apparent wind
27.5 knots
at 21° angle

Boat speed 16 knots

21°

Velocity triangle upwind in 14 knots true wind.
Optimum angle might be slightly further off the
wind to become fully foilborne.

required foil area is surprisingly small. The foil configuration is 'aeroplane', with the main load carried forward and a light-laden controlling tailplane aft. The main difficulty with the foils is keeping inside the maximum width allowed by the class rules. To achieve this the hulls and crossbeams do not take up the full allowance of beam, since the foils will be providing full-width stability once the craft is foilborne. For speed sailing there is no beam restriction, however, and alternative front foils with a wider beam would be used for record attempts.

The sailing qualities would only be found by experiment. Calculations show that aerodynamic cleanness has a special advantage in producing large forward forces from wing rigs even in quite low true wind strengths. The resultant force produced by air flow over a wing builds up as the square of its velocity, and the apparent wind may be used to produce increasing power as the boat speeds up. This means, in effect, that the boat creates its own wind. This is where the hydrofoil advantage comes into its own: in a conventional craft drag increases rapidly, even for the slender hulls of a catamaran, at speeds above 15 knots. However when foilborne the hydrofoil drag increases only a little over the range of 15 to 35 knots and the foils will thus match the performance of the rig. This phenomenon is similar to that found in ice yachts, which regularly sail at four to five times wind speed. Although this level of performance is not reached on water, a foil equipped C Class cat should remain foilborne except when tacking and gybing, in true winds of around 10 knots and upwards. Supporting evidence of this may be adduced from recent 'orthodox' C Class designs, in which it is possible to fly a hull with both crew fully extended in true winds over 8 knots.

Using the apparent wind in this way, in ultra-high performance sailing craft, is best understood by means of velocity triangle diagrams for sailing downwind, reaching and sailing upwind (see page 105). They show that the apparent wind will always come from well ahead, except while tacking and gybing. That C Class cats already produce this performance is shown by their crews fully extended on trapezes, with one hull flying, on the 45° downwind tacks.

Speed sailing with a hydrofoil converted C Class cat will be relatively easy, compared with racing round a triangular Olympic course. The advantages of aero- and hydrodynamic cleanness will also apply, and it is likely that only around 20 knots of true wind will be required for record attempts, giving an advantage in reducing wave height and the effects of gusts. The objective would lie not only in gaining the C Class World Sailing Speed Record, but also in attempting the outright record. Close contact with the current Little America's Cup challenge of John Downie may lead to foil conversion of a C Class cat in the near future.

The hydrofoil conversion of *Catapult* is the least ambitious, in technical terms, on the list of untried projects. *Catapult* is the same size as *Mayfly* and the foil configuration and design would be very similar. Although not purpose-built for foil conversion, *Catapult* has features of particular suitability: the inflatable hulls are very light and their extra load once foilborne would thus be less. As the hulls are of relatively poor hydrodynamic design, because of limitations in the shape that can be produced as an inflatable structure, there will be a further advantage in being rid of hull drag at speeds above 10–12 knots. In addition, and this is speculative, there is an opportunity to return to the original idea of a 'dis-posable' hull. For this purpose the hulls could be inflated within wide rubber straps, and a large release valve would allow quick deflation once foilborne. A small compressed air cylinder would provide quick reflation at the end of a tack or speed run. The current *Catapult* hulls would probably present *greater* aerodynamic drag if deflated in this way once foilborne, but a certain elegance in the idea makes it irresistible – in theory.

Catapult also has favourable features in her framework and rig. The frame is robustly made for the commercial market, and strong points necessary for hydrofoil attachment are easily found. The rig has evolved through various stages, benefiting from advances in sailboard design. The boat is thus provided with a rig of between 8 and 10 sq m, of considerable aerodynamic efficiency and capable of standing high apparent winds without distortion. All these features would give *Catapult* some advantage over the original *Mayfly*, and be likely to generate speeds around 30 knots. Alas, this speed is no longer relevant to world records in the appropriate classes, since both 10 sq m and A Class world records are already held at considerably higher speeds by sailboards of one sort or another. However, *Catapult* would not require the physical fitness and skill necessary for speed sailing on sailboards, and the project would be attainable on a very modest budget. Development of the foil design could allow for speeds of over 30 knots, especially by reducing the dimensions of the foil tips front and back. This would be in line with the tiny foil areas required to produce the necessary lift, and might give *Catapult* a truly remarkable turn of speed, in addition to good seakeeping properties in waves up to a foot high.

Third on the list of untried projects comes the foil

Catapult looks very suitable for foil conversion.

conversion of a large offshore multihull, such as the arrangements I suggested for *Colt Cars* in 1983. The main problem of such a venture is to find the resources necessary to design and structure the foils, in addition to finding a 'willing' owner. The largest successful sailing hydrofoils so far are *Williwaw*, *Monitor* and *Icarus II*. Up to the size of these craft the resources required are not huge, and such projects can be justified simply as innovations. Once above 40 ft overall length, however, the cost of developing hydrofoils will be so great that a defined objective must be identified in advance. In the mid-1980s resources of this size were applied to the development of numerous multihulls, mainly sponsored and built in France. The objective would be to capture the high level of media interest given to offshore multihull events. The sponsor often sees a large return in television time within a few months of the craft being completed. No sponsor has yet been convinced that a gamble on a *flying* hydrofoil is worth taking, although stabilisation by foils has been widely used.

What are the advantages and disadvantages in attempting to convert a large light-weight offshore multihull to hydrofoils? The main advantage is an increase in speed, in appropriate conditions, and the second advantage is the 'cushioned' ride in small or moderate sized waves. A hydrofoil craft can 'platform' with its flying height greater than the wave height, and 'contour' or follow the waves when they are larger (see diagram overleaf). These modes of behaviour have been well worked out for powered hydrofoils in the open sea, but a hydrofoil converted multihull will have an advantage not shared by powered craft: the hulls are slender and will cut through wave tops, even at high speed, without producing unacceptable drag. There is therefore an intermediate mode

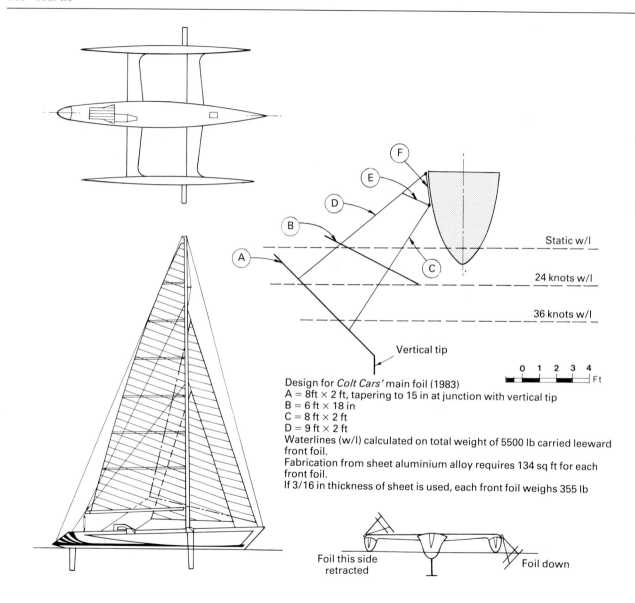

Colt Cars' foils
were designed after
a day spent on
board with Rob and
Naomi James. They
have not been built.

Static w/l

24 knots w/l

36 knots w/l

Vertical tip

Design for *Colt Cars'* main foil (1983)
A = 8ft × 2 ft, tapering to 15 in at junction with vertical tip
B = 6 ft × 18 in
C = 8 ft × 2 ft
D = 9 ft × 2 ft
Waterlines (w/l) calculated on total weight of 5500 lb carried leeward
front foil.
Fabrication from sheet aluminium alloy requires 134 sq ft for each
front foil.
If 3/16 in thickness of sheet is used, each front foil weighs 355 lb

0 1 2 3 4
Ft

Foil this side
retracted

Foil down

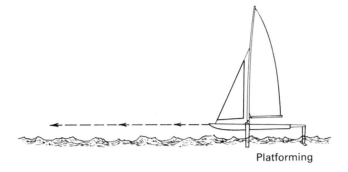

Platforming

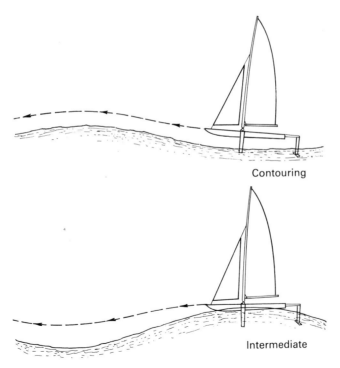

Contouring

Intermediate

between platforming and contouring where hydrofoils will greatly improve speed and stability despite the hulls themselves cutting some wave tops. The greater the 'flying height' the greater will be the chance of staying foilborne in increasing waves, and in this one area 'the bigger the better' will apply to the craft itself; flying height will be approximately related to overall size, although hydrofoil configuration and design will play a part.

The disadvantages of any large hydrofoil craft, apart from cost, concern first the Cube Law, second light-wind performance and third uncertain behaviour in big seas. The Cube Law phenomena will be tackled first. If a small model or prototype is used for testing and then scaled up, the strength of any given structure or support goes up only as the square of a given dimension, while the weight or load goes up as the cube. It is thus deceptively easy to make models strong enough for a given purpose and find full sized counterparts hopelessly too weak. Nature provides examples of this scaling effect, and it is only necessary to consider the different ratio of leg thickness to body for an insect and an elephant to realise the magnitude of the problem – and this is before asking the elephant to jump many times its own height in a fraction of a second, a task the insect does with ease. This problem of supporting large structures may well have limited animal size in evolution, and possibly contributed to the demise of the dinosaurs. Each increase in hydrofoil size will produce formidable structural and engineering problems. In addition there is deterioration of the power to weight ratio, unless precautions are taken, since sail area increases only as the square of a given dimension, while the structural load increases as the cube in the manner described above. These problems were solved successfully in *Icarus II*, and the use of modern materials in the enterprising hands of multihull designers such as John Shuttleworth, Nigel Irens and Adrian Thompson has also reduced their effect. By comparing the power to weight ratios for various craft including the small hydrofoils (see diagram) it is seen that there is ample power in relation to weight for flying in modern large multihull designs.

During 1983 I explored likely openings, spending a day on *Colt Cars* with Rob and Naomi James and another on *Elf Aquitaine*. Recent designs such as

Apricot, Paragon and the Formula 40s are even more suitable for hydrofoil conversion, but the resource problem remains unsolved. The final disadvantage, concerning the range of wind and sea conditions in which foils would confer advantage, can only be determined by experiment. Many of the arguments are similar to those for the C Class cat. Sailing across the wind in any conditions except light airs, foils would improve performance sometimes dramatically. Going to windward there is a question mark, although they would probably improve performance over quite a range of favourable conditions. Downwind is likely to mean a series of 45° tacks, as with the Tornado or C Class boats, with a real chance of staying foilborne in moderate and strong winds because of the increased apparent wind, as described earlier. In light airs, on all points of sailing the foils will be retracted since they would otherwise produce unacceptable drag. Even the extra load represented by the foils tipped over on deck may diminish light air performance to some extent, and a tradeoff between advantages and disadvantages over a range of conditions will occur. In relation to the various high publicity events, it may be that the Lerwick to Lowestoft leg of the Round Britain Race represents the best bet. This leg is often a beam reach in conditions not quite as severe as the open ocean, since the land mass of Britain gives protection from the most usual westerly winds. Retractable hydrofoils must by their nature be shipped and unshipped readily, and an enterprising competitor might allow the necessary small lugs and fittings to be installed on the boat before the race, with the foils themselves only shipped aboard for a favourable leg. By this means the buildup of confidence in hydrofoil performance might proceed in stages.

Power/weight ratio of various craft, in relation to their weight.

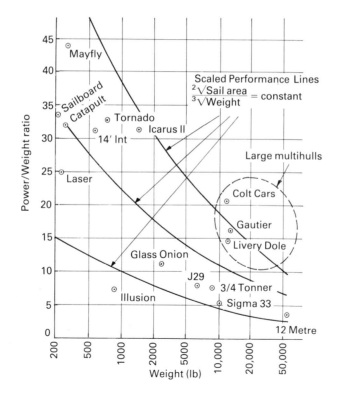

Fourth on the list of projects is the sailboard. At this end of the size scale the resources required to make foils are tiny, and they can be hand-wrought in metal or composites with ease. A number of experimenters, myself included, have made hydrofoil boards which have flown, but none have produced a turn of speed worth mention. One reason for this failure is that shown in the table: none of the designs have allowed for the small foil areas involved, i.e. the required area to carry the all-up load at 20 knots is 0·6 sq ft and at 40 knots only one-quarter of this. There is difficulty in contemplating foils as small as this, but some idea is given by imagining a table knife held edge-on in the water alongside a fast motorboat. The knife is then angled a few degrees and, provided ventilation is efficiently controlled by fences (small fins around the blade), a large force is readily generated. The knife analogy also indicates that the foils, however small, will still need to run deep to get below surface interference. Speed attempts by sailboards are often dogged by wavelets 3 to 6 in high, and a foil system which provides stable flight at this height above the water might find a place. There is no requirement for wide lateral stability, and a possible foil system would be in under the board, occupying the same area as the skeg on normal speed boards. There is a safety aspect to this, since the sailor should not be put at risk of falling into the water in front of a knife-edge foil system running at over 30 knots. Speed sailors are not at present injured by their own skegs, and would not be put at risk by a foil system in this position. The problem of balancing on a single slender strut would be no more difficult than skating or riding a bicycle, and fore-and-aft stability is provided by the hydrofoil tailplane. Flying height is set by controlled ventilation: as the controlling fence clears the water surface, air passes down onto the lifting surfaces and reduces lift. Once this fence is reimmersed the air is instantly washed off and full lift restored.

Fifth on the list is the updating of *Icarus* for the purpose of challenging an orthodox Tornado in a race round-the-buoys. No comparison of speed has ever been made either straight upwind or straight downwind. On the reaching legs *Icarus* has an 8 knot advantage (*Icarus* 28 knots, the Tornado 20 knots), but this might be offset by the difficulties of going upwind and down. Development of the Tornado rig works in favour of foils, since more power means more speed which gives a better chance of reaching the crossover point on the drag curve. Close-windedness of the hydrofoil craft might be slightly less than the orthodox Tornado, but the extra speed generated by the foils should more than compensate for this. On the downwind leg the *Icarus* team would require practice in running as far offwind as possible while staying foilborne; expert Tornado sailors develop such skills to maintain a high apparent wind on downwind legs. To validate the comparison it

Lift produced by 'practical hydrofoils' at different speeds

Speed		Lift	
10 knots	= 5·16 m/sec	57 lb/sq ft	= 279 kg/sq m
15	7·74	128	626
20	10·3	228	1115
25	12·9	356	1740
30	15·5	513	2510
35	18·0	698	3415
40	20·6	912	4464

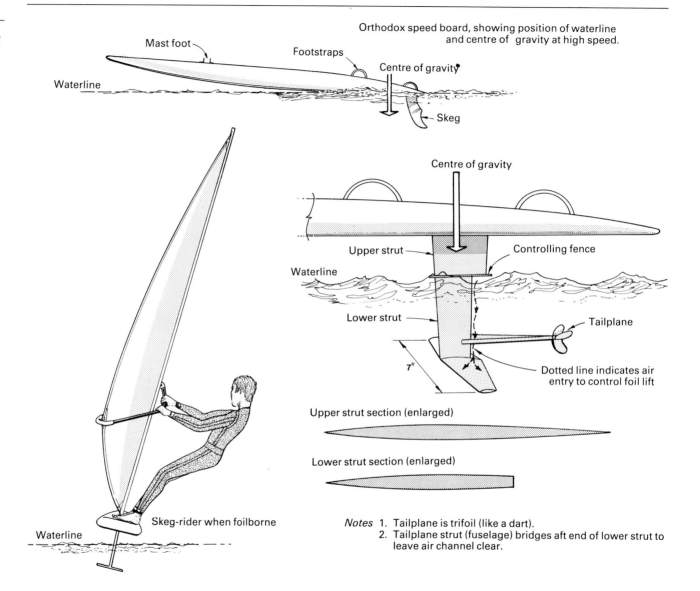

Foilborne 'Skeg-rider', a high-speed hydrofoil conversion of a sailboard.

Orthodox speed board, showing position of waterline and centre of gravity at high speed.

Mast foot

Footstraps

Centre of gravity

Waterline

Skeg

Centre of gravity

Upper strut

Controlling fence

Waterline

Lower strut

Tailplane

7"

Dotted line indicates air entry to control foil lift

Upper strut section (enlarged)

Lower strut section (enlarged)

Skeg-rider when foilborne

Waterline

Notes 1. Tailplane is trifoil (like a dart).
2. Tailplane strut (fuselage) bridges aft end of lower strut to leave air channel clear.

would be necessary to set up *Icarus* and the standard Tornado with identical rigs, and swap crews between alternate races.

The sixth hydrofoil project is the conversion of *Crossbow II* to foils. This might seem like an instant dinosaur, and likely to suffer rapid extinction, but the opposite is the case. Foils are at their best when straight-line reaching speed in calm water is the order of the day, and the higher the takeoff speed the more certain that the ultimate speed will be raised. The foil area for takeoff at 30 knots is 8·8 sq ft, assuming a total weight of 2 tons, and the foils could be attached to external beadings in a similar manner to *Icarus* and *Icarus II*. The reduction in drag would be huge, since it has been estimated that *Crossbow II* pulls along an envelope of water equal to half her own displacement, in view of her large wetted area. The only problems likely to be encountered at above 40 knots concern cavitation, which occurs when the negative pressure on the upper surface of the foil exceeds atmospheric pressure and a vapour cavity is created on the upper surface so that the water effectively boils there. Cavitation is avoided by not overloading the foils, and by using a 'delayed cavitation' foil section. The overall loading on *Crossbow II* would be much reduced by hydrofoil conversion, and she would be in a position to regain her world record from the sailboard. This would be a fairly low cost project since only the foils and their attachments require construction.

The last project is based on a blank cheque: what would be the features of a purpose-built, money-no-object, sailing hydrofoil? My answer is based on the conviction that hydrofoil sailing in the open sea is possible in wind and sea conditions between Forces 3 and 7. A multihull approximately 60 ft long would

Russian hydrofoil design that delays cavitation and reduces ventilation.

be used as a floating testbed to evaluate and compare various surface piercing and incidence controlled foils. Methods of controlling flying height would include 'planned ventilation' of surface piercing struts, and sonic echo from the water surface with computer damping for foil incidence control. Recent advances in rig design and the use of synthetic composite materials would be incorporated, and the objective would be to outsail the conventional fast offshore multihulls whenever there was sufficient wind to be foilborne. By this means hydrofoil development would take over some of the huge resources being applied to offshore multihull racing, and in addition the World Sailing Speed Record might be won, finally, by a hydrofoil equipped sailing craft.

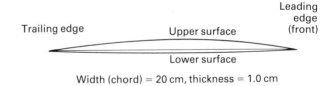

Width (chord) = 20 cm, thickness = 1.0 cm

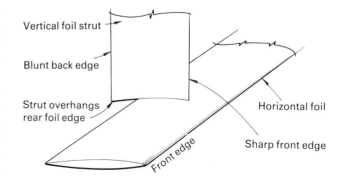

APPENDIX

World Sailing Speed Records and Classes

Classes

Based on International Yacht Racing Union sail area
sizes for multihulls

Unlimited Class: sail area over 27·88 sq m
C Class: from 21·84 to 27·88 sq m
B Class: from 13·94 to 21·84 sq m
A Class: from 10·0 to 13·94 sq m
10 Square Metre Class: from 8·0 to 10·0 sq m
8 Square Metre Class: up to 8 sq m

World Records held in 1987

Unlimited Class: Pascal Maka, sailboard   38·9
knots   1986
C Class: *Jacob's Ladder*   25·0 knots   1982
B Class: *Icarus*   28·1 knots   1985
A Class: Serge Griesseman and Manu Bertin,
tandem sailboard   35·1 knots   1986
10 Sq M Class: Griesseman and Bertin   34·9 knots
1986
8 Sq M Class: Pascal Maka   38·9 knots 1986

Icarus' Hydrofoils   1969–87

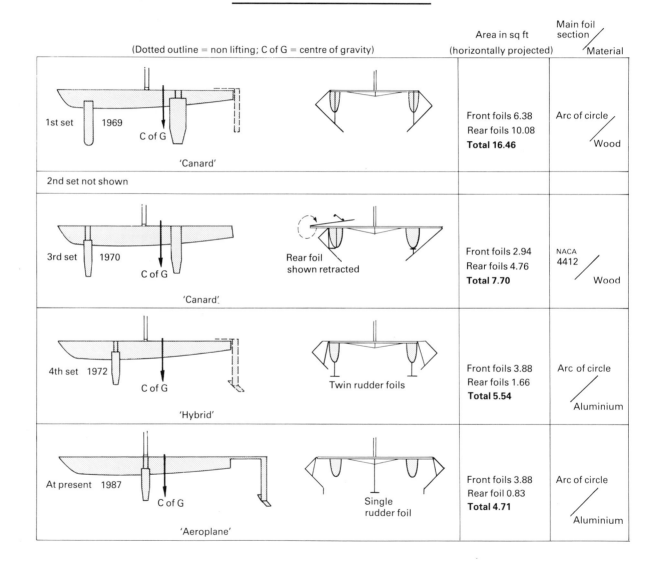

	Area in sq ft (horizontally projected)	Main foil section / Material
(Dotted outline = non lifting; C of G = centre of gravity)		
1st set 1969 C of G 'Canard'	Front foils 6.38 Rear foils 10.08 **Total 16.46**	Arc of circle / Wood
2nd set not shown		
3rd set 1970 C of G 'Canard' Rear foil shown retracted	Front foils 2.94 Rear foils 4.76 **Total 7.70**	NACA 4412 / Wood
4th set 1972 C of G 'Hybrid' Twin rudder foils	Front foils 3.88 Rear foils 1.66 **Total 5.54**	Arc of circle / Aluminium
At present 1987 C of G 'Aeroplane' Single rudder foil	Front foils 3.88 Rear foil 0.83 **Total 4.71**	Arc of circle / Aluminium

Hydrofoil Lift Calculations

by Dr Alan Alexander

$$\text{Lift} = 2\cdot77\ U^2\ S\ C_L \qquad\qquad (A)$$
$$L = \text{lift in pounds}$$
$$U = \text{speed in knots}$$
$$S = \text{foil area in sq ft}$$

The lift coefficient C_L is taken from experimental data reports and an average value at the maximum lift: drag ratio is $0\cdot5$.

But surface effect and aspect ratio losses require correction by the factor

$$0\cdot9 \times \frac{A}{A+2} \qquad \left(A = \text{aspect ratio} = \frac{(\text{Length})^2}{\text{Area}} \right)$$

In addition the lift will be related to the horizontally projected area, requiring the planform area of the foil to be corrected by the cosine of the dihedral angle ($\cos \theta$).

Thus the lift derived from the immersed part of a practical surface-piercing hydrofoil, in the absence of ventilation, is:

$$\text{Lift} = 2\cdot49\ U^2\ S\ \frac{A}{A+2}\ \cos\theta \qquad (B)$$

The dihedral angle and aspect ratio of a given foil, at a stated immersion depth, are determined in advance; but of the three variables lift, speed and area, two may be known and the formula used to find the unknown.

For example, what speed does *Icarus* require to complete takeoff (called U_t), with her present foils? And what speed is required for her to clear the support strut (called U_c), in flat water?

Assumptions: main foils carry 80% of total load
leeward front foil carries 80% of front foil load
total load = 700 lb

Calculation is thus based on a load on the leeward front foil of:

$$700 \times 0\cdot8 \times 0\cdot8 = 448\ \text{lb}.$$

Planform of immersed foil at takeoff is:

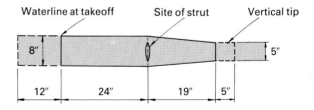

The vertical tip contributes no lift but adds 5 in of length and 25 sq in of area to aspect ratio calculations.

To calculate takeoff speed U_t:

area (as planform) = 2·19 sq ft
aspect ratio = 6·78
substituting in formula B:

$$448 = 2·49 \times U_t{}^2 \times 2·19 \times \frac{6·78}{8·78} \times \cos 45°$$

$$\therefore U_t{}^2 = \frac{448}{2·79}$$

$\therefore$ takeoff speed U_t = 12·3 knots

To calculate speed to clear support strut, U_c:

area (from strut downwards) = 0·85 sq ft
aspect ratio = 3·89
substituting in formula B:

$$448 = 2·49 \times U_c{}^2 \times 0·85 \times \frac{3·89}{5·89} \times \cos 45°$$

$$\therefore U_c{}^2 = \frac{448}{0·99}$$

Speed to clear strut U_c = 21·3 knots.

Both speeds accord with the available evidence from photos and timed runs, but no on-board speed meter has ever been used. At speeds above 21·3 knots the waterline moves further towards the foil tip, and small waves can be encountered without the strut passing through them.

Drag Analysis of Sculling Hydrofoil

The drag of practical hydrofoils, when attached to craft, is given by Hoerner:

$$D = \tfrac{1}{2}\rho \times v^2 sc \times 0{\cdot}016 + \frac{2L^2}{\pi \tfrac{1}{2}\rho v^2 s^2}$$

where c = chord of foil in metres
    s = span or maximum width in metres
    v = velocity in m/sec
    L = load (or lift) of boat, foils and sculler, in kg
    ρ = density of water (102 Tekma/cu. m)

In this equation Hoerner has doubled the drag coefficient (0·016) in the first half of the equation, representing profile drag, to allow for parasitic drag from 'supports, spray, rudder and propulsion parts'. A typical section value for the NACA 4412 is half of this (0·008). Similarly in the second half of the equation, representing induced drag, he has doubled the theoretical value to account for 'biplane effect, downwash, wave drag, additional section drag due to lift, and induced strut interference'.

It may be seen from the phrases quoted that a variety of the factors mentioned do not apply to the sculling hydrofoil, specifically the 'rudder, propulsion parts and biplane effect'. The one factor which may be greater than his allowances is surface proximity drag, but this can be reduced to a low value by designing any fully immersed horizontal foil to run more than one chord length below the surface. The data for the sculling hydrofoil are: loaded weight 90 kg, velocity 4·6 m/sec, main foil span 1·5 m, chord 0·1 m. The average load carried by the main foil is 85% of the total. The front foil will function less efficiently because of surface effect losses. If the front foil produces 20% more drag for each kilogram of lift, then the total drag is increased by 3%. Substituting these values in the equation above gives a total drag of 4·7 kg (profile drag 2·6 kg + induced drag 2·1 kg). No allowance has been made for air drag, which is by no means negligible, but the doubling factors of Hoerner are available to offset this and any other unquantified extras. On the basis of these assumptions the required horsepower for steady flight is 0·29 on flat water. Some information is available on the delivered horsepower of an oarsman in a racing shell eight in a 2,000 m race, and it has been found to be 0·347 hp (National Physical Laboratory (NPL) Ship Division Report 1967, by Wellcome). Thus the sculler will have something in reserve in travelling 2,000 metres on foils at the speed required to win at Henley. The author attempted to verify this drag reduction in a simple experiment: two equally loaded sculling boats, one with foils one without, were towed side by side behind a motorboat with the towing lines interconnected round pulleys. It was intended to measure the difference in drag by means of a spring balance attached to a loop in the middle of the towing line. The experiment proved difficult because of a minor misalignment of the sculling hydrofoils and accurate readings of drag reduction were thus not obtained, but for short periods of time the drag of the foilborne boat was less than the one without foils.

Apparent Wind Angle (β) as Summation of Aero- and Hydro-dynamic Drag Angles

Aerodynamic resultant R_1 = Hydrodynamic resultant R_2

$\quad a \;$ = aerodynamic drag angle

$\quad \gamma \;$ = hydrodynamic drag angle

$\quad \beta \;$ = $a + \gamma$ (by simple geometry)

Thus a reduction in either drag angle contributes equally to reducing β and increasing performance.

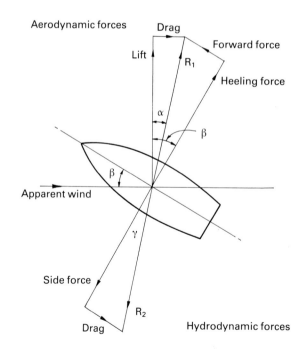

Icarus II

List of Owners

Anderson, John
Botham, Russell (*Seafly*)
Bye, Tony (*Seafly*)
Casson, Ted
Douglas, Colin (*Seafly* and Swann Hunter Training
   & Safety Co.)
Fowler, John
Green, Andrew
Grogono, Alan
Grogono, Bernard
Grogono, James
Howard, Alan (I.Y.E.)
Lessware, Derek (Sarma U.K.)
Mitchell, John
Pearce, Terry (I.Y.E.)
Sample, Brian (*Seafly*)

Component Weights

2 Hulls @ 220	440 lb	
2 Front foils @ 80	160	
2 Masts @ 65	130	
Rear beam	67	
Rear foil beam	41	
Rear foil	40	
Front beam	36	
High level crossbeam	29	
Rear foil mount	15	
Booms, rigging etc	105	
Sails	52	
Total	1115 lb = $\frac{1}{2}$ ton (507 Kg)	

(Note: individual items were weighed on bathroom scales, total checked on weighbridge.)

Bibliography

Books

Theory of Wing Sections, I. Abbott and A. von Doenoff. Dover Publications, New York 1949
Fluid Dynamic Drag, S. Hoerner. Published by the author, Box 342, Brick Town, NJ, USA 1957
Sailing Hydrofoils, AYRS Members. Amateur Yacht Research Society 1970
Hydrofoil Sailing, A.J. Alexander, J.L. Grogono, D.J. Nigg. Published Juanita Kalerghi, London 1972
Aero-Hydrodynamics of Sailing, C. Marchaj. Adlard Coles Ltd, London 1979
Gossamer Odyssey, M. Grosser. Houghton Mifflin, Boston 1980
An Album of Fluid Motion, M. Van Dyke. Parabolic Press, Stanford, California 1982
Faster Faster, D. Pelly. Nautical Books, London 1984
Mechanics of Fluids, A. Walsham and D. Jobson. Longmans, London 1979

Articles by the author

'Up up and away', *Yachts and Yachting* Oct. 1969
'Apparent wind', *Yachts and Yachting* May 1970
'The Little America's Cup', *Yachting World* Oct. 1970
'Purpose-built foil-cat', *Yachts and Yachting* Jan. 1971
'Foiled again', *Yachting World* Dec. 1971
'Flying feline' *Yachts and Yachting* Feb. 1972
'Three on foils', *Yachts and Yachting* Sept. 1972
'Sailing speed record attempts', *Hydrofoil and Hovering Craft* Oct. 1972 and Dec. 1973
'How to make a cat fly', *Practical Boat Owner* May 1973
'Get your hydrofoils right', *Yachting World* July 1974
'*Mayfly*: a sailing hydrofoil development', *RINA Journal* July 1977
'*Icarus II*', *Yachts and Yachting* Sept. 1977
Speed trials – reports each November in *Yachts and Yachting* 1977–82
'Sculling hydrofoil', *Yachts and Yachting* March 1979

'*Dots*, a 7 kg speedboard', RINA Small Craft
Symposium Oct. 1981
'Large sailing hydrofoils', High Speed Surface Craft
Conference Papers May 1983
'Sculling hydrofoil', RINA Small Craft Symposium
Nov. 1984

Other articles

Speed Week reports. D. Pelly in *Yachting World*
each November 1972–6 and *Yachts and Yachting*
each November 1983–6
'Design and development of a man-powered
hydrofoil', M. Brewster. BSME Thesis, M.I.T. 1979
'Development of a human powered racing hydrofoil',
D. Owers. RINA Small Craft Symposium 1984
'An investigation into the feasibility of a human
powered rowing hydrofoil', G. Charlton, C.P.R.
Penman, A. Millward. *International Shipbuilding
Progress* Feb. 1987

Index